W9-CHV-052

THE ENCYCLOPEDIA OF PSYCHOACTIVE DRUGS

SERIES 1

The Addictive Personality
Alcohol and Alcoholism
Alcohol: *Customs and Rituals*
Alcohol: *Teenage Drinking*
Amphetamines: *Danger in the Fast Lane*
Barbiturates: *Sleeping Potions or Intoxicants?*
Caffeine: *The Most Popular Stimulant*
Cocaine: *A New Epidemic*
Escape from Anxiety and Stress
Flowering Plants: *Magic in Bloom*
Getting Help: *Treatments for Drug Abuse*
Heroin: *The Street Narcotic*
Inhalants: *The Toxic Fumes*

LSD: *Visions or Nightmares?*
Marijuana: *Its Effects on Mind & Body*
Methadone: *Treatment for Addiction*
Mushrooms: *Psychedelic Fungi*
Nicotine: *An Old-Fashioned Addiction*
Over-The-Counter Drugs: *Harmless or Hazardous?*
PCP: *The Dangerous Angel*
Prescription Narcotics: *The Addictive Painkillers*
Quaaludes: *The Quest for Oblivion*
Teenage Depression and Drugs
Treating Mental Illness
Valium: *and Other Tranquilizers*

SERIES 2

Bad Trips
Brain Function
Case Histories
Celebrity Drug Use
Designer Drugs
The Downside of Drugs
Drinking, Driving, and Drugs
Drugs and Civilization
Drugs and Crime
Drugs and Diet
Drugs and Disease
Drugs and Emotion
Drugs and Pain
Drugs and Perception
Drugs and Pregnancy
Drugs and Sexual Behavior

Drugs and Sleep
Drugs and Sports
Drugs and the Arts
Drugs and the Brain
Drugs and the Family
Drugs and the Law
Drugs and Women
Drugs of the Future
Drugs Through the Ages
Drug Use Around the World
Legalization: *A Debate*
Mental Disturbances
Nutrition and the Brain
The Origins and Sources of Drugs
Substance Abuse: *Prevention and Treatment*
Who Uses Drugs?

PRESCRIPTION
NARCOTICS

EDITOR, WRITER
OF UPDATED MATERIAL
Ann Keene

GENERAL EDITOR
OF UPDATING PROJECT
Professor Paul R. Sanberg, Ph.D.
*Department of Psychiatry, Neurosurgery,
Physiology, and Biophysics
University of Cincinnati College of Medicine; and
Director of Neuroscience, Cellular Transplants, Inc.*

GENERAL EDITOR
Professor Solomon H. Snyder, M.D.
*Distinguished Service Professor of
Neuroscience, Pharmacology, and Psychiatry at
The Johns Hopkins University School of Medicine*

ASSOCIATE EDITOR
Professor Barry L. Jacobs, Ph.D.
*Program in Neuroscience, Department of Psychology,
Princeton University*

SENIOR EDITORIAL CONSULTANT
Jerome H. Jaffe, M.D.
*Director of The Addiction Research Center,
National Institute on Drug Abuse*

THE ENCYCLOPEDIA OF PSYCHOACTIVE DRUGS

PRESCRIPTION NARCOTICS

The Addictive Painkillers

WITHDRAWN

PAUL R. SANBERG, Ph.D.

Ohio University

MICHAEL D. BUNSEY

Cornell University

CHELSEA HOUSE PUBLISHERS

NEW YORK   PHILADELPHIA

Chelsea House Publishers

EDITOR-IN-CHIEF: Remmel Nunn
MANAGING EDITOR: Karyn Gullen Browne
PICTURE EDITOR: Adrian G. Allen
ART DIRECTOR: Maria Epes
MANUFACTURING MANAGER: Gerald Levine
SYSTEMS MANAGER: Lindsey Ottman
PRODUCTION MANAGER: Joseph Romano

THE ENCYCLOPEDIA OF PSYCHOACTIVE DRUGS

EDITOR OF UPDATED MATERIAL: Ann Keene

STAFF FOR PRESCRIPTION NARCOTICS: THE ADDICTIVE PAINKILLERS

PRODUCTION EDITOR: Marie Claire Cebrián
LAYOUT: Bernard Schleifer
APPENDIXES AND TABLES: Gary Tong
PICTURE RESEARCH: Diane Wallis, Sandy Jones

UPDATED 1992
3 5 7 9 8 6 4 2

Library of Congress Cataloging-in-Publication Data
Sanberg, Paul.
    Prescription narcotics.
    (The Encyclopedia of psychoactive drugs)
    Bibliography: p.
    Includes index.
    Summary: Explores the use of prescription narcotics, the risks and
consequences of addiction, and current treatments.
    1. Narcotic habit—Juvenile literature.   2. Narcotics—Toxicology—Juvenile
literature.   3. Narcotic habit—Treatment—Juvenile literature.   [1. Narcotic
habit.   2. Drugs.   3. Drug abuse]   I. Title.   II. Series.
RC566.S23   1986   616.86'3   86–1283

ISBN 0-87754-770-X
    0-7910-0771-5 (pbk.)

Photos courtesy of AP/Wide World Photos, Art Resource, Museum of the City of
New York, New York Public Library, UPI/Bettmann Archive.

CONTENTS

FOREWORD 9

INTRODUCTION 13

1. Getting Hooked 19
2. Pain 25
3. The History of the Opiates 31
4. The Effects of Narcotics on the Body 39
5. The Endogenous Opiates 49
6. Prescriptions for Narcotics 59
7. The Treatment of Narcotics Addiction 79
8. The Challenge Today 89

APPENDIX I: Population Estimates of Lifetime and
Current Nonmedical Drug Use, 1988 92

APPENDIX II: Drugs Mentioned Most Frequently by
Hospital Emergency Rooms, 1988 94

APPENDIX III: Drugs Mentioned Most Frequently by
Medical Examiners (in Autopsy Reports), 1988 95

APPENDIX IV: National High School Senior Survey,
1975–1989 96

APPENDIX V: Percentage of High School Seniors
Reporting Any Illicit Drug Use, 1975–1989 98

APPENDIX VI: Drug Abuse and AIDS 98

APPENDIX VII: U.S. Drug Schedules 100

APPENDIX VIII: Agencies for the Prevention and
Treatment of Drug Abuse 101

FURTHER READING 106

GLOSSARY 107

INDEX 110

A sign strategically placed near a New York City graveyard emphasizes the deadly potential of narcotics abuse. With many prescription narcotics, there is a thin line between effective and lethal doses.

FOREWORD

Since the 1960s, the abuse of psychoactive substances—drugs that alter mood and behavior—has grown alarmingly. Many experts in the fields of medicine, public health, law enforcement, and crime prevention are calling the situation an epidemic. Some legal psychoactive substances—alcohol, caffeine, and nicotine, for example—have been in use since colonial times; illegal ones such as heroin and marijuana have been used to a varying extent by certain segments of the population for decades. But only in the late 20th century has there been widespread reliance on such a variety of mind-altering substances—by youth as well as by adults.

Day after day, newspapers, magazines, and television and radio programs bring us the grim consequences of this dependence. Addiction threatens not only personal health but the stability of our communities and currently costs society an estimated $180 billion annually in the United States alone. Drug-related violent crime and death are increasingly becoming a way of life in many of our cities, towns, and rural areas alike.

Why do people use drugs of any kind? There is one simple answer: to "feel better," physically or mentally. The antibiotics your doctor prescribes for an ear infection destroy the bacteria and make the pain go away. Aspirin can make us more comfortable by reducing fever, banishing a headache, or relieving joint pain from arthritis. Cigarettes put smokers at ease in social situations; a beer or a cocktail helps a worker relax after a hard day on the job. Caffeine, the most widely

used drug in America, wakes us up in the morning and over-
comes fatigue when we have exams to study for or a long
drive to make. Prescription drugs, over-the-counter remedies,
tobacco products, alcoholic beverages, caffeine products—
all of these are legally available substances that have the capacity to change the way we feel.

But the drugs causing the most concern today are not
found in a package of NoDoz or in an aspirin bottle. The
drugs that government and private agencies are spending
billions of dollars to overcome in the name of crime prevention, law enforcement, rehabilitation, and education have
names like crack, angel dust, pot, horse, and speed. Cocaine,
PCP, marijuana, heroin, and amphetamines can be very dangerous indeed, to both users and those with whom they live,
go to school, and work. But other mood- and mind-altering
substances are having a devastating impact, too—especially
on youth.

Consider alcohol: The minimum legal drinking age in all
50 states is now 21, but adolescent consumption remains
high, even as a decline in other forms of drug use is reported.
A recent survey of high school seniors reveals that on any
given weekend one in three seniors will be drunk; more than
half of all high school seniors report that they have driven
while they were drunk. The average age at which a child has
his or her first drink is now 12, and more than 1 in 3 eighth-
graders report having been drunk at least once.

Or consider nicotine, the psychoactive and addictive ingredient of tobacco: While smoking has declined in the population as a whole, the number of adolescent girls who smoke
has been steadily increasing. Because certain health hazards
of smoking have been conclusively demonstrated—its relationship to heart disease, lung cancer, and respiratory disease;
its link to premature birth and low birth weight of babies
whose mothers smoked during pregnancy—the long-term effects of such a trend are a cause for concern.

Studies have shown that almost all drug abuse begins in
the preteen and teenage years. It is not difficult to understand
why: Adolescence is a time of tremendous change and tur-
moil, when teenagers face the tasks of discovering their iden-
tity, clarifying their sexual roles, asserting their independence
as they learn to cope with authority, and searching for goals.
The pressures—from friends, parents, teachers, coaches, and

one's own self—are great, and the temptation to want to "feel better" by taking drugs is powerful.

Psychoactive drugs are everywhere in our society, and their use and misuse show no sign of waning. The lack of success in the so-called war on drugs, begun in earnest in the 1980s, has shown us that we cannot "drug proof" our homes, schools, workplaces, and communities. What we can do, however, is make available the latest information on these substances and their effects and ask that those reading it consider the information carefully.

The newly updated ENCYCLOPEDIA OF PSYCHOACTIVE DRUGS, specifically written for young people, provides up-to-date information on a variety of substances that are widely abused in today's society. Each volume is devoted to a specific substance or pattern of abuse and is designed to answer the questions that young readers are likely to ask about drugs. An individualized glossary in each volume defines key words and terms, and newly enlarged and updated appendixes include recent statistical data as well as a special section on AIDS and its relation to drug abuse. The editors of the ENCYCLOPEDIA OF PSYCHOACTIVE DRUGS hope this series will help today's adolescents make intelligent choices as they prepare for maturity in the 21st century.

Ann Keene, Editor

A U.S. military orderly makes a medicinal compound by mixing assorted drugs. The Civil War provided the first opportunity for the widespread application of such opiate narcotics as morphine.

USES AND ABUSES

Jack H. Mendelson, M.D.
Nancy K. Mello, Ph.D.
Alcohol and Drug Abuse Research Center
Harvard Medical School—McLean Hospital

Human beings are endowed with the gift of wizardry, a talent for discovery and invention. The discovery and invention of substances that change the way we feel and behave are among our special accomplishments, and like so many other products of our wizardry, these substances have the capacity to harm as well as to help.

Consider alcohol—available to all and recognized as both harmful and pleasure inducing since biblical times. The use of alcoholic beverages dates back to our earliest ancestors. Alcohol use and misuse became associated with the worship of gods and demons. One of the most powerful Greek gods was Dionysus, lord of fruitfulness and god of wine. The Romans adopted Dionysus but changed his name to Bacchus. Festivals and holidays associated with Bacchus celebrated the harvest and the origins of life. Time has blurred the images of the Bacchanalian festival, but the theme of drunkenness as a major part of celebration has survived the pagan gods and remains a familiar part of modern society. The term *Bacchanalian festival* conveys a more appealing image than "drunken orgy" or "pot party," but whatever the label, some of the celebrants will inevitably start up the "high" escalator to the next plateau. Once there, the de-escalation is often difficult.

According to reliable estimates, 1 out of every 10 Americans develops a serious alcohol-related problem sometime in his or her lifetime. In addition, automobile accidents caused by drunken drivers claim the lives of more than 20,000 people each year, and injure 25 times that number. Many of the victims are gifted young people just starting out in adult life. Hospital emergency rooms abound with patients seeking help for alcohol-related injuries.

Who is to blame? Can we blame the many manufacturers who produce such an amazing variety of alcoholic beverages? Should we blame the educators who fail to explain the perils of intoxication or so exaggerate the dangers of drinking that no one could possibly believe them? Are friends to blame— those peers who urge others to "drink more and faster," or the macho types who stress the importance of being able to "hold your liquor?" Casting blame, however, is hardly constructive, and pointing the finger is a fruitless way to deal with problems. Alcoholism and drug abuse have few culprits but many victims. Accountability begins with each of us, every time we choose to use or to misuse an intoxicating substance.

It is ironic that some of our earliest medicines, derived from natural plant products, are used today to poison and to intoxicate. Relief from pain and suffering is one of society's many continuing goals. More than 3,000 years ago, the Therapeutic Papyrus of Thebes, one of our earliest written records, gave instructions for the use of opium in the treatment of pain. Opium, in the form of its major derivative, morphine, remains one of the most powerful drugs we have for pain relief. But opium, morphine, and similar compounds, such as heroin, have also been used by many to induce changes in mood and feeling. Another example of a natural substance that has been misused is the coca leaf, which for centuries was used by the Indians of Peru to reduce fatigue and hunger. Its modern derivative, cocaine, has important medical use as a local anesthetic. Unfortunately, its increasing abuse in recent years has reached epidemic proportions.

The purpose of this series is to provide information about the nature and behavioral effects of alcohol and drugs and the probable consequences of their use. The authors believe that up-to-date, objective information about alcohol and drugs will help readers make better decisions about the wisdom of their use. The information presented here (and in other books in this series) is based on many clinical and laboratory studies and observations by people from diverse walks of life.

Over the centuries, novelists, poets, and dramatists have provided us with many insights into the effects of alcohol and drug use. Physicians, lawyers, biologists, psychologists, and social scientists have contributed to a better understanding of the causes and consequences of using these substances. The authors in this series have attempted to gather and condense all the latest information about drug use. They have also described the sometimes wide gaps in our knowledge and have suggested some new ways to answer many difficult questions.

How, for example, do alcohol and drug problems get started? And what is the best way to treat them when they do? Not too many years ago, alcoholics and drug abusers were regarded as evil, immoral, or both. Many now believe that these persons suffer from very complicated diseases involving deep psychological and social problems. To understand how the disease begins and progresses, it is necessary to understand the nature of the substance, the behavior of the afflicted person, and the characteristics of the society or culture in which that person lives.

The diagram below shows the interaction of these three factors. The arrows indicate that the substance not only affects the user personally but the society as well. Society influences attitudes toward the substance, which in turn affect its availability. The substance's impact upon the society may support or discourage the use and abuse of that substance.

Although many of the social environments we live in are very similar, some of the most subtle differences can strongly influence our thinking and behavior. Where we live, go to school and work, whom we discuss things with—all influence our opinions about drug use. Yet we also share certain commonly accepted beliefs that outweigh any differences in our attitudes. The authors in this series have tried to identify and discuss the central, most crucial issues concerning drug use.

In 1853, Dr. Alexander Wood developed the hypodermic syringe in the hope that its use would reduce the chances of drug abuse. Unfortunately, the injection of drugs became widely prevalent among addicts.

Regrettably, human wizardry in developing new substances in medical therapeutics has not always been paralleled by intelligent usage. Although we do know a great deal about the effects of alcohol and drugs, we have yet to learn how to impart that knowledge, especially to young adults.

Does it matter? What harm does it do to smoke a little pot or have a few beers? What is it like to be intoxicated? How long does it last? Will it make me feel really fine? Will it make me sick? What are the risks? These are but a few of the questions answered in this series, which we hope will enable the reader to make wise decisions concerning the crucial issue of drugs.

Information sensibly acted upon can go a long way toward helping everyone develop his or her best self. As one keen and sensitive observer, Dr. Lewis Thomas, has said,

> *There is nothing at all absurd about the human condition. We matter. It seems to me a good guess, hazarded by a good many people who have thought about it, that we may be engaged in the formation of something like a mind for the life of this planet. If this is so, we are still at the most primitive stage, still fumbling with language and thinking, but infinitely capacitated for the future. Looked at this way, it is remarkable that we've come as far as we have in so short a period, really no time at all as geologists measure time. We are thè newest, the youngest, and the brightest thing around.*

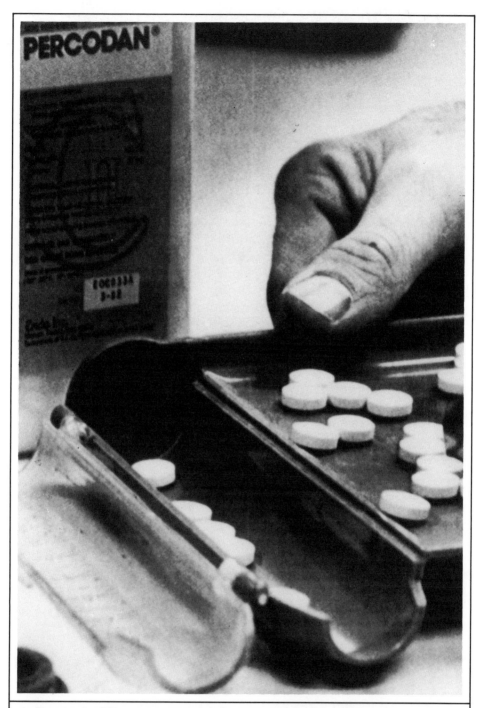

A pharmacist filling a prescription for Percodan tablets. Percodan produces roughly the same analgesic (painkilling) effect as morphine.

CHAPTER 1

GETTING HOOKED

Susan's experience with drugs started off innocently enough. When she was a sophomore in college, she was introduced to the drug Percodan by her dentist, who prescribed the painkiller to decrease the discomfort caused by extensive root canal work. Susan took the prescribed amount of the drug and promptly discontinued its use when her pain lessened. However, she did not forget the pleasant effects produced by the drug. A few years later, while working for a major corporation, Susan was introduced to a coworker named Bill. He was a close friend of a local doctor and was thus able to get an unlimited supply of cheap Percodan, which he persuaded Susan to use. In the end, however, Susan paid a high price for using the drug—$3 per tablet and five years of her life. Her habit became more and more expensive as her dosage gradually rose from one tablet a day to over a dozen.

Susan's heavy use of Percodan did not destroy her ability to work. In fact, she felt her best while under the influence of the drug and was able to move steadily up the corporate ladder. The occasional mental cloudiness and loss of concentration produced by the drug was never detected by her superiors. Even when she took double doses—which never failed to make her dizzy and once caused her to faint—her coworkers never associated her behavior with drug use. To them she remained a model employee.

Under this facade of success, however, Susan began having doubts about her own stability. When she experienced occasional bouts of nausea and vomiting, she began to suspect that what she had once regarded as a harmless habit had grown to be a real problem. What worried her even more was her first blackout. She had only taken a few pills that day, but the half-bottle of wine she consumed that same evening had put her out like a light. When she awakened on the floor, she discovered her scrapes and bruises. After that she tried not to mix alcohol and Percodan, but it was sometimes difficult to pass up an occasional drink.

The dimensions of Susan's problem became more apparent after she had been promoted to a position that involved considerable traveling. The new position provided her with the opportunity to meet new people, see new places—and find new dentists. Susan would present these dentists with her old dental X-rays and plead: "Since my dentist back home is scheduled to work on my teeth in just a few weeks, could you please give me something to ease the pain until then?" This ploy usually worked, enabling Susan to acquire the Percodan and continue her habit. In addition, she began altering the numbers on the dentists' prescriptions to ensure a limitless supply.

Despite her rapidly growing drug problem, Susan's career continued to advance and she soon earned yet another promotion. On the surface things appeared to be more promising than ever. This time, however, Susan's job did not involve traveling, and for the first time Percodan was not readily obtainable. In the absence of the drug, Susan finally realized what a crutch it had become. On those days when she was unable to secure a fix, she suffered from anxiety, insomnia, and various aches and pains. Her frequent yawning, runny nose, sweatiness, and goose bumps were explained to friends as signs of a cold. But she realized that this lifestyle could not continue. Unable to cope without Percodan—but determined to rid herself of her dependency on it—Susan decided to quit her job and enter a drug rehabilitation program. It proved to be a very wise decision.

The Opiate Narcotics

Natural and synthetic opiates make up the class of drugs known as the narcotic analgesics. Natural opiates are those drugs that are extracted from the seed capsules of the opium poppy, *Papaver somniferum.* Synthetic opiates are drugs that are made from chemicals and that have psychological and physiological effects that are similar to those of the natural opiates. An analgesic is a drug that kills pain without causing loss of consciousness. And a narcotic is a type of drug that depresses the nervous system and produces effects similar to those of morphine, such as sedation and a pleasant state of euphoria. (Although both marijuana and cocaine have been legally and popularly classified as narcotics, they technically are not.)

The opiate narcotics have been a mixed blessing in the annals of medicine. Throughout history their remarkable analgesic effects have relieved the suffering of countless numbers of people. In 1680 Thomas Syndenham, the English physician who was the founder of clinical medicine and the first to introduce opium into medical practice, proclaimed that "among the remedies which it has so pleased Almighty God to give to man to relieve his suffering, none is so universal and so efficacious as opium."

The ability of opium to reduce pain, coupled with its ability to induce euphoria, has given it universal popularity. Elizabeth Barrett Browning, Charles Baudelaire, Théophile Gautier, Alexandre Dumas, Edgar Allan Poe, and Samuel Taylor Coleridge were all users of the opium preparation laudanum. In fact, Coleridge wrote his brilliant poem "Kubla Khan" while in an opium reverie. However, the pleasurable effects that laudanum brought these artists came only at the cost of long dry spells in their creativity and the occasional loss of ambition. More important, to achieve the analgesic and euphoric effects, they inevitably risked overdose and addiction.

Though the possibility of overdose does exist for the opiate user, the true curse of narcotics use is the threat of addiction. Too often the use of an analgesic, while successfully alleviating the intense pain of illness or injury, creates an equally debilitating chemical dependence. That is why one of the primary goals of many scientists today is the development of a narcotic analgesic that has no addictive properties. Such a drug would have an almost unimaginable impact on society. Millions of people would be safely relieved of their pain, and thousands more would be saved from addiction. Furthermore, the lives of the addicts' families and friends would improve as well. In addition, if the drug were legal and relatively inexpensive, addicts would no longer have to resort to criminal acts to support their habits and crime rates across the nation would plummet. Thus, although researchers now know little about the actions of the opiates, future study holds great hope.

Even with an incomplete understanding of the opiates, if people used narcotics properly, they could minimize the damage caused by the drugs. To clarify this, it might be helpful to define "drug use," "drug misuse," and "drug abuse." Drug use is ingesting a drug for its intended purpose and in the appropriate dosage and frequency. Although even proper use of a narcotic does not guarantee freedom from addiction, at

The English poet Elizabeth Barrett Browning (1806–61) regularly used laudanum, a highly addictive preparation containing opium, to help her cope with the pain of a childhood spinal injury that left her an invalid for the rest of her life.

present it is the best way to reduce its incidence. Drug misuse is using a drug for its intended purpose but taking it in greater amounts or more frequently than recommended. This practice tends to lead to addiction. Because opiates produce effects that make people feel the more they take, the less they hurt, these drugs are often overprescribed by the doctor and overused by the patient. This increases the risk of dependence. Finally, drug abuse is the deliberate use of a drug for a reason other than its intended purpose and in doses and frequencies that are potentially damaging to the user. Narcotics abuse often arises from innocent misuse that later becomes intertwined with addiction.

Thus, one preliminary step in reducing addiction is for doctors to closely monitor narcotics prescriptions and to avoid giving out these drugs whenever possible. The more this can be done, the more we can minimize drug misuse and the accidental addiction that so often befalls the patient who is in pain.

The French poet and critic Charles Baudelaire (1821–67) was another prominent writer who used laudanum. His Les Paradis Artificiels (The Artificial Paradises) *was based on his own drug experiences. Baudelaire also translated into French the works of Edgar Allan Poe (1809–49), yet another occasional user of laudanum.*

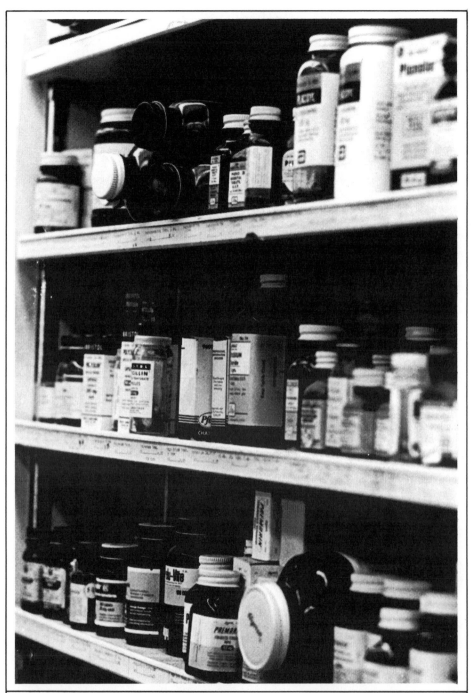

According to a scale established by the U.S. Controlled Substances Act, most prescription narcotics fall within the Schedule II and Schedule III classifications, meaning that these drugs have a high abuse potential.

CHAPTER 2

PAIN

*T*o better understand narcotics, it is important to have some knowledge of pain—the universally dreaded symptom that these drugs work to eliminate. Although at present little is known about how the opiates reduce pain, current research on narcotics, pain, and the brain has provided many fascinating new insights into the causes of pain and the methods of alleviating it.

Pain is essential to a person's existence in that it acts as a warning system, alerting an individual to possible damage to the body. For example, it tells us not to touch a hot stove or cuddle a porcupine. Without the ability to feel pain, by the time a person reached adolescence he or she would most likely be covered by networks of scars and burns. In fact, this is what has occurred in those rare cases of people who were born without the ability to feel pain. Finally, because of pain's function as a warning system, it is also one of the most important symptoms a physician can use in diagnosing disease.

There are two basic ways to classify pain. The first focuses on the subjective experience of pain, describing it as either sharp and quick or slow and dull. Narcotics are more successful in blocking the latter type of pain, such as that usually associated with illness. However, high doses of narcotics can also block the sharper, quicker pain. Pain can also be classified as being either somatic or visceral. Somatic pain occurs in the skeletal muscles or bones, whereas visceral pain arises from nonskeletal parts of the body such as the intestines or stomach. Narcotics have proven most useful in alleviating visceral pain.

Interestingly, pain is closely related to emotion. Because pain and emotion are localized in the same part of the brain, pain can be intertwined with our feelings in a manner unlike any other sensation. Consequently, pain—especially slow, deep pain such as that associated with the intestines—is often accompanied by an emotional response, such as depression and anxiety, in addition to a physiological response, such as sweating and nausea.

Pain has a number of other peculiar characteristics. One involves what is known as *phantom pain*, a sensation that is

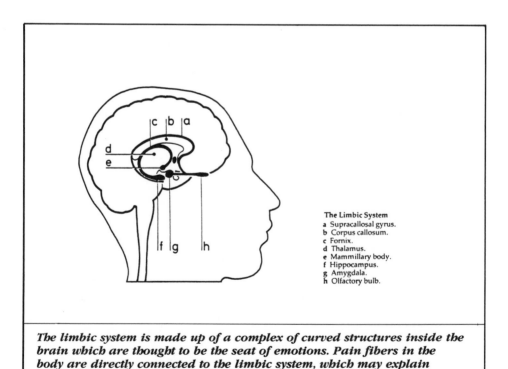

The Limbic System
a Supracallosal gyrus.
b Corpus callosum.
c Fornix.
d Thalamus.
e Mammillary body.
f Hippocampus.
g Amygdala.
h Olfactory bulb.

The limbic system is made up of a complex of curved structures inside the brain which are thought to be the seat of emotions. Pain fibers in the body are directly connected to the limbic system, which may explain emotional reactions to physical injury.

often experienced by amputees. The patient experiencing phantom pain might feel a dull throbbing in his right "foot" even though the leg has been removed. Another interesting aspect of pain is its relationship to age. In general, older people are less sensitive to pain than younger people. Awareness of pain is also related to personality type. As a rule, introverts are more sensitive to pain than extroverts. This is probably because introverts are more focused on themselves and their bodily sensations and thus tend to notice pain more. Pain perception is also related to such things as time of day (sensitivity increases as the day goes on) and even hair color (redheads are the most sensitive and brunettes the least sensitive to pain).

Finally, one's sensitivity to pain is affected by shock, stress, anger, environment, outlook, and societal and attitu-

Nineteenth-century French physicians observe a colleague placing a patient under the influence of a hypnotic trance. Hypnosis, an induced state resembling sleep, can sometimes block the sensation of pain.

dinal factors. In addition, hypnotic trance can entirely block the sensation of pain. Why can some members of certain religious groups smile as their backs are whipped until they bleed? It is this great variability of pain sensation that has encouraged scientists to study the body's internal painkilling (analgesia) system.

The Biology of Pain

To understand this analgesia system, one must first examine the biology of pain. The surface of the human body is completely covered with nociceptors, or pain receptors. However, the nociceptors are not distributed evenly throughout the body. For example, they are much more dense in the fingertips than in the back. These receptors can detect coldness, warmth, touch, and, with intense stimulation, pain. The nociceptors all reside on neurons, or nerve cells, that ultimately communicate with the brain. When these receptors are exposed to intense stimuli, the neurons to which they are attached are activated and send more information to the brain. This information is interpreted as pain.

A hospital during the Civil War. Morphine addiction became known as the "soldier's disease" in the late 1800s because many wounded soldiers who were treated with morphine for pain became addicted to the drug.

There are at least two types of pain fibers, or chains of nerves, that carry the pain signals. The A-delta fibers carry the sharp, quick pain and the C-fibers carry the slow, dull pain—the type that narcotics are especially successful in blocking. Both types of fibers communicate with the thalamus (the part of the brain that is sometimes described as a pain-signal terminal that sends the pain message to other parts of the brain), the cerebral cortex (the outermost area of the brain, which is the seat of consciousness and the center of memory, learning, reasoning, judgment, and intelligence), and, interestingly, the limbic system (thought to be a center for emotions). This direct connection to the limbic system might explain the emotional aspects of pain that were mentioned earlier.

Until recently, researchers had no idea how pain is stopped. Throughout history, this lack of knowledge has hampered the efforts of doctors to eliminate pain without inducing adverse side effects. Physicians have been limited to giving drugs that either are unable to stop the pain sufficiently or replace the pain with addiction, an equally damaging alternative. The lack of understanding of pain has made it extremely difficult to manipulate or alleviate it, a major problem that doctors frequently encounter. The search for an understanding of pain and its control is closely linked with the history of the opiates themselves.

The medicinal use of opiate narcotics dates to ancient times. Galen, the 2nd-century C.E. Greek writer and one of antiquity's most eminent physicians, used opium to alleviate his patients' pain.

CHAPTER 3

THE HISTORY OF THE OPIATES

*T*he earliest evidence of the medicinal use of opiate narcotics is in the writings of Theophrastus, a 3rd century B.C.E. (Before the Common Era, equivalent to B.C.) Greek philosopher who studied under Aristotle. At that time, the opiates were administered through punctures in the skin or inhaled as a vapor. Ingested in this way, the drugs produced extremely inconsistent results, ranging from insufficient analgesia to coma and death. In the 2nd century C.E. the Greek physician Galen used opium to relieve his patients' suffering. Approximately 700 years later, the Arab physicians Al Rhazi and Avicenna also employed opium preparations. With the subsequent occupation of Spain by the Moors (descendants of Arabs and Berbers), knowledge of the medicinal uses of opium spread. Early in the 16th century the Swiss physician Paracelsus created laudanum, an opium preparation that is still in use. By the 17th century opium was widely used for medicinal purposes throughout Europe.

Arab traders transported opium to China as early as 800 C.E., where it was initially used to control dysentery. However, its medicinal use gradually turned to recreational abuse, and by the late 1600s opium smoking had become rampant. In 1729 opium smoking was outlawed in China, and the punishment for the crime was strangulation. Soon afterwards, the importation of opium from India, China's major supplier, was forbidden. However, the powerful British East India Company, which was in charge of importing the drug, refused to cease its opium operations. The continued smuggling of the drug, coupled with China's continued resistance, led to the Opium War (1839–42) between Great Britain and China. A second so-called Opium War was waged from 1856 to 1860.

The widespread use of opium by the Chinese soon had an impact on the United States, which imported thousands of Chinese laborers to help build the great western railroads in the middle of the 19th century. It was inevitable that use of the drug would spread to the general population. In addition, a number of other factors contributed to the escalation of American opiate abuse, which peaked at the turn of the century. Among these was the extraction of opium's active ingredient, morphine (named after Morpheus, the Greek god of dreams), by the German chemist Frederick Serturner. This extract was 10 times more potent than opium itself. The discovery of morphine led to further research on

The writings of Theophrastus, a 3rd-century B.C.E. Greek scientist, contain the earliest mention of the medicinal use of opiates, which were at that time administered either through skin punctures or inhaled as a vapor.

opium, and in 1832 a second compound was extracted—codeine. The discovery of these substances roughly coincided with the development of the hypodermic syringe by Alexander Wood in 1853. Ironically, Wood perfected the syringe in hopes of reducing the chances of addiction linked with opiate use. Today it is known that the injection of a drug greatly *increases* the addictive potential of opiates.

In the 1860s the Civil War afforded the first opportunity for the widespread application of the new knowledge of the opiates. Morphine injections were used to treat pain, dysentery, and fatigue in both Confederate and Union soldiers. Unfortunately, however, abuse of the drug was not uncommon. In fact, morphine addiction became known as the "soldier's disease."

But addiction was not confined to the battlefield, as many people, particularly women, soon found out. Patent medicines, which could be easily purchased through the mail or over-the-counter at the local drugstore, usually contained

The Swiss physician and alchemist Paracelsus (1493–1541) pioneered the use of chemicals in treating disease. In the early 16th century he introduced an alcoholic solution of opium that he named "laudanum."

opium derivatives—a fact not usually known by the consumer. These drugs, often advertised as being effective in reducing menstrual pain, greatly appealed to women, who quickly became addicted. Equally disturbing is the fact that many children and babies were given the opiate medicines. The most popular of these medicines was paregoric, an opium-based tincture that was used (and is still used) to treat diarrhea in small children. Because the opium also had a noticeable calming effect on the child, many mothers were encouraged to continue administering the drug. Addiction was an inevitable result.

By 1900 the combination of these factors—the importation of Chinese laborers, the development of morphine and the syringe, the Civil War, and the easy accessibility of patent medicines—had led to a major opiate addiction problem in the United States. There were as many as 1 million addicts, and 3 out of every 4 were women. Indeed, the typical addict of the time could best be described as a middle-aged Southern white woman, who was a caring wife and a responsible

In March 1839, Chinese authorities tried to stop the illegal opium trade by destroying 20,000 chests of British-owned opium, an action that triggered the Opium Wars between China and England.

mother—hardly the picture of a drug addict that usually comes to mind. In 1906, as a first step in battling the danger of the patent medicines, the Federal Pure Food and Drug Act was passed. It required that medicines containing opiates be plainly labeled to that effect. This legislation resulted in a significant decline in the abuse of opiates.

Strangely enough, the street addict, as generally perceived today, did not begin to flourish until there was a major technological "advance" that modified the morphine molecule to form a supposedly safer opiate. The new drug was a would-be cough medicine called Heroin, named for the drug's presumably "heroic" ability to produce the effects of morphine without causing addiction. Unfortunately, heroin turned out to be anything but nonaddictive.

The heroin addict is often stereotyped as a young male living in an inner-city neighborhood and coming from an oppressed ethnic group. He has typically been introduced to

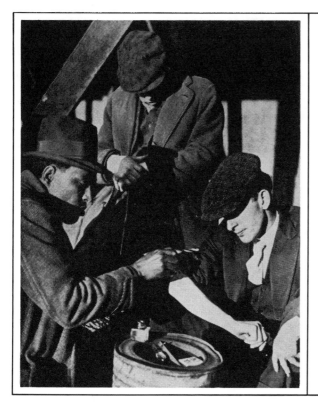

Heroin was originally marketed as a cough medicine and cure for morphine addiction. However, abuse of the drug soon became widespread, resulting in an increasing number of street addicts such as these American junkies in the 1920s.

the drug by friends who share his feelings of depression, futility, and hopelessness. The addict is probably attracted to the opiate's power to replace these negative feelings with those of peace and repose, to extinguish worries and to induce a coolly detached state.

In reality, heroin addiction cuts across all social, racial, and occupational boundaries. Opiate abuse among doctors and nurses involves the medicinal opiates and arises from different needs and desires than those of the street addict. Since they are in a very high pressure occupation and have easy access to opiates, it should not be surprising that many medical professionals abuse these substances. One study concluded that 15% of all narcotics addicts were in the medical profession, a figure greater than that for any other occupation. However, in contrast to the street narcotics abuser, these addicts can usually continue to function well, as they have access to clean, sterile equipment and untainted drugs, and know how to use them.

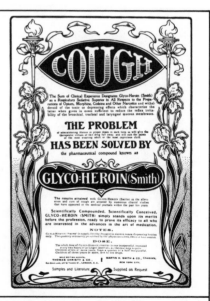

Six 19th-century advertisements for opiate medicines. It was initially thought that heroin could produce the effects of morphine without causing addiction. This soon proved to be untrue, and in the mid-1920s the manufacture of heroin in the United States was prohibited.

Some do not fare so well, however. For example, one Michigan dentist eventually lost his license after becoming addicted to Demerol, a strong prescription narcotic that is commonly abused by physicians. This man often jerked convulsively while extracting teeth, costing him both patients and assistants. One day, a physician found the dentist collapsed on the floor of his office. The doctor treated the dentist's track-mark infections, produced by the use of syringes, and neither man reported the incident. The next time such an incident occurred, the dentist lost his license.

Not all narcotics addicts fall into these two broad categories. Many addicts resemble the patent-medicine victims of the late 1800s. Initially receiving doctors' prescriptions for drugs to treat true ailments yet ignorant of the potentially dangerous properties of these substances, these individuals become inexorably drawn into the net of addiction.

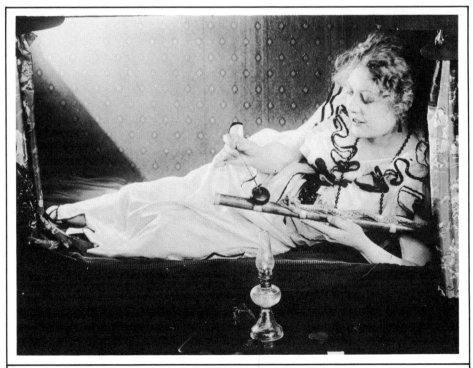

By 1900 nearly a million Americans were addicted either to opium or its derivatives, and three out of every four addicts were women.

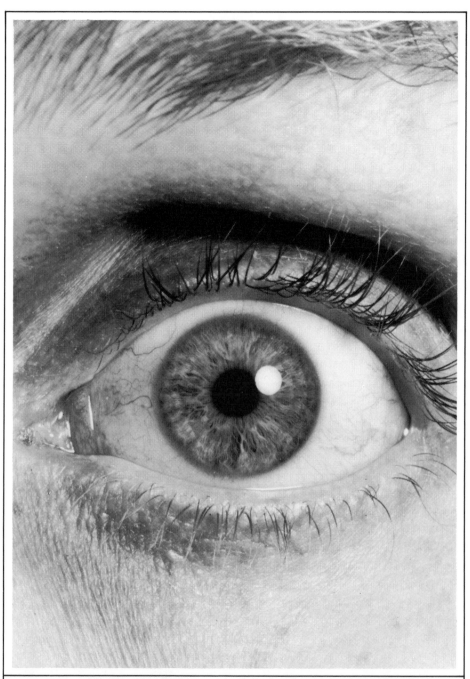

Moderate doses of narcotics such as opium, morphine, or heroin produce contracted or "pinpoint" pupils. Police often check the eyes of a person suspected of being under the influence of these drugs for pupil constriction, one of the few overt signs of opium addiction.

CHAPTER 4

THE EFFECTS OF NARCOTICS ON THE BODY

*N*arcotics are central nervous system depressants that relieve pain without causing loss of consciousness. They can also produce feelings of drowsiness, mental confusion, and euphoria. On the other hand, a normal, healthy person who experiments with narcotics may initially feel dysphoric, which is characterized by a general feeling of being unwell and/or unhappy.

The analgesic effect of narcotics results, in part, from the drugs' effects on the emotional aspects of pain. Many patients experiencing pain have attested that after the administration of a narcotic, their pain is as intense as ever but no longer as bothersome. This phenomenon can be explained by the unique relationship between pain and emotion. Because narcotics block the negative emotional effects associated with pain, they make it much more bearable.

Narcotics produce this effect by reducing anxiety and apprehension and decreasing the perceived aversion to the pain. This is possible because of pain's peculiar nature. For example, the anxiety related to the expectation of pain associated with going to the dentist is closely related to how intensely the pain is felt. Thus, morphine, which minimizes the negative emotional aspects of pain, is more effective at blocking pathological pain (such as pain from a serious illness), which is a high-anxiety type of pain, than experimentally induced pain, which can be thought of as a low-anxiety type of pain. (In the latter case, the "victim" knows that the pain is temporary and meaningless.)

However, the relationship between anxiety and pain is not quite so simple. Anxiolytics, or anti-anxiety drugs, are ineffective analgesics. If narcotics alleviated pain merely by reducing anxiety, the anti-anxiety drugs would be just as effective. Apparently, then, the painkilling effect of narcotics is due to some relationship between the deadening of the pain sensation, the suppression of anxiety, and some other factor or factors, such as changes in the recognition of pain or changes in the memory or judgment that follow the recognition of pain. The analgesic effect of narcotics is also almost certainly related to the positive feelings, such as euphoria and a general sense of contentment and pleasure, that accompany the use of these drugs and increase a person's ability to tolerate pain. In addition, these same feelings may be responsible for the reduction in cravings for food and sex that usually accompanies the heavy use of opiate narcotics.

Other Physiological Effects

Analgesia and euphoria are not the opiates' only effects. In moderate doses these drugs decrease sensitivity to most internal and external stimuli (including, of course, pain), lower inhibition, and, as previously mentioned, reduce anxiety. In addition, moderate doses produce muscle relaxation and pupil constriction. Indeed, police often look for "pinpoint" pupils in individuals suspected of using narcotics. Opiates can also induce vomiting. Perhaps the narcotics' most dangerous effect on the central nervous system is respiratory depression. Narcotics desensitize the respiratory center in the brain, which regulates breathing by constantly monitoring the amount of carbon dioxide in the blood. Consequently, the brain signals the lungs to slow down. The decreased breathing caused by a moderate dose of narcotics is usually not a problem. However, when coupled with the respiratory effects of another central nervous system depressant, such as alcohol, a moderate narcotics dose can be fatal. Mixing narcotics with other depressants is perhaps the primary danger involved in the use of these drugs. This is even a problem in the hospital, where narcotics can produce an adverse effect when combined with anesthetics during surgery.

Moderate doses of narcotics also impair the ability to concentrate. Therefore, it is hazardous to drive or work with potentially dangerous equipment while under the influence of these drugs. In addition, the opiates' depressive effect produces a dreamy, restless sleep.

Several of the body's regulatory systems are also affected by moderate doses of narcotics. These drugs increase the tone of the bladder sphincter, making urination difficult. Similarly, the digestive system's action in the stomach and intestines is slowed, resulting in constipation. Thus, opiates are sometimes used as antidiarrheals (remedies for diarrhea). Unfortunately, the body builds up tolerance to this effect, and, even worse, if after a prolonged period of opiate use the individual stops taking the drug, diarrhea will result. This is due to what is known as the *rebound effect*, the appearance of a symptom that is the opposite of the drug's normal effect and the result of the sudden cessation of drug use. This phenomenon, associated with the prolonged use of many drugs,

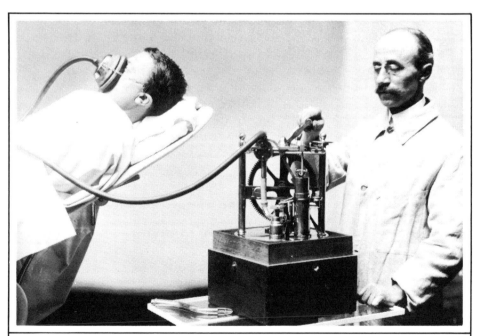

This turn-of-the-century device administered chloroform through inhalation. Introduced as a general anesthetic in 1847, chloroform was once a common form of surgical anesthesia, but it is seldom used today.

is caused by the body reacting as if the drug were still present. However, because it is not, the body overcompensates and produces opposite effects.

Besides their use as antidiarrheals, opiates, especially codeine, are also valued for their antitussive, or cough-suppressant, ability and have been included in a number of cough medicines. In the past, the availability of these medicines made them attractive to young people who experiment with drugs. Consequently, codeine was removed from many of these over-the-counter remedies. However, over 40 prescription cough medicines still contain codeine.

Even slightly higher than moderate doses of a narcotic produce additional effects. The euphoria, often called a "kick" or "rush," usually becomes marked and can be accompanied by elation in individuals who are either abnormally depressed or highly excited. On the other hand, healthy, pain-free individuals often experience unpleasant feelings. These higher doses also cause more nausea and vasodilation, or an increase in the diameter of the blood vessels. This latter effect can be of use in clearing the lungs and improving the breathing of certain patients, but it can also be harmful, because the increased blood flow causes a rise of pressure in the brain. This can be especially dangerous for persons with head injuries. Vasodilation can also cause rapid decreases in blood pressure, resulting in dizziness and fainting.

At the highest doses, opiates can be extremely dangerous. Pupil constriction, one of the few signs of opiate use, becomes more evident and respiratory rate goes down even further, sometimes resulting in unconsciousness. However, unlike many other drugs, even at very high doses narcotics do not produce marked effects on coordination or speech. Because of this, many individuals who are using the highest doses of narcotics can still function in society.

The Effects of Long-Term Narcotics Use

After long-term narcotics use, the picture changes. Although long-term narcotics use has not been linked to permanent physical or psychological degeneration, it can result in weight loss, frequent infection, and a decrease of sex hormones. Ironically, the analgesic effect of narcotics becomes a liability in long-term use because it can cause the user to be unaware of injuries and disease. But the most important—and dreaded—consequence of long-term narcotics use is addiction. Though some people can use the opiates indefinitely without becoming addicted, for most this is not the case.

Drug addiction has been divided into two distinct categories—psychological dependence and physical dependence—both of which can be induced by narcotics. Psychological dependence is a condition in which the drug user craves a drug to maintain a sense of well-being and feels discomfort when deprived of it. The picture of a street addict robbing a store to get money for a fix may spring to mind,

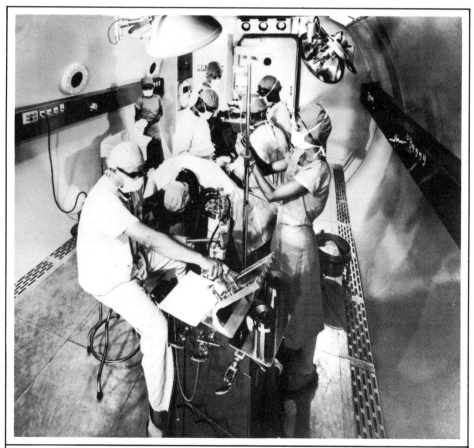

Operating room at New York's Mount Sinai Hospital. Because both opiate narcotics and surgical anesthesia depress the respiratory system and slow down the breathing rate, these drugs can be dangerous if combined.

but dependence can just as easily be seen in the businessman wheedling his doctor for a bigger prescription. Physical dependence is an adaptive state of the body to the presence of a drug. It is marked by intense physical disturbance when drug use is stopped. This disturbance is called withdrawal.

Withdrawal

Withdrawal symptoms may be mild or severe, though they are rarely life-threatening. The severity of withdrawal depends primarily upon the degree of dependence and the abruptness of drug cessation. Generally, a patient taking up to 80 mg (milligrams) of morphine daily for up to one month will not risk severe withdrawal when the dosage is discontinued. However, tripling the amount of morphine and continuing administration for over a month will almost certainly result in painful withdrawal once drug use is stopped. These numbers are guidelines only—individual differences are important in determining how much of a drug reaches its target, how much accumulates in the body, how the drug reacts with other drugs and foods, and how quickly it is metabolized and eliminated.

Though the nature of narcotics withdrawal depends upon which narcotic is used, the typical withdrawal is long and painful, setting in hours after the final drug dose and lasting up to seven days or more. For morphine withdrawal, the first symptoms, which strike approximately six hours after the last dose, are drug craving and anxiety. About eight hours later, yawning, perspiration, and a runny nose appear, followed by pupil dilation, goose bumps, and muscle twitches. These symptoms are also accompanied by appetite loss, muscle aches, and hot and cold flashes. Within a day or so, all of the above symptoms intensify. In addition, there will be insomnia, nausea, fever, increased blood pressure, and a quickened pulse. Shortly thereafter, the previously mentioned symptoms again increase, and there is the appearance of vomiting, diarrhea, and arm and leg flailing. In addition, the individual may sometimes assume the fetal position. In short, it is a most agonizing ordeal and one that seems to the sufferer to last forever. Most of these symptoms disappear completely within a week or two, but there is apparently a secondary phase of withdrawal, which is characterized by irritability, muscle aches, and gradually decreasing levels of insomnia and which may last for up to six months after the last dose.

For a narcotic such as methadone, which has a much slower, milder initial effect than morphine, the withdrawal can last much longer but be less severe. Methadone withdrawal does not start until one to two days after the last dose is taken. The more severe symptoms, such as fever and nausea, usually do not appear until at least three days after the last dose, and the last primary symptoms may continue for up to six or seven weeks.

Environmental factors often affect dependence and withdrawal. The procedures and rituals associated with narcotics use, such as preparing and injecting the drug, are reinforcing and come to play a role in the physiological effects of the

An average dose of prescription narcotics causes drowsiness and affects concentration, making driving while under their influence dangerous.

narcotic. For example, when laboratory rats are subjected to withdrawal in a certain cage and months later are returned to the same cage, they re-experience the withdrawal symptoms. Human addicts also show withdrawal symptoms when they return to the site of former abuse. However, dependence and withdrawal are primarily a direct result of changes in the user's body chemistry. Consequently, it is these changes that are of greatest interest.

Tolerance

One important result of prolonged narcotics use is tolerance, a phenomenon common to the use of many drugs. Defined simply, tolerance is the decreasing effectiveness of a drug after repeated use. In other words, higher and higher doses of the drug are needed to bring about its original effect. In the case of most of the opiates, tolerance develops very rapidly. It takes the form of shorter and less intense analgesia, sedation, and euphoria, as well as a significant increase in the dose required to cause death. In addition, many narcotics, because of their similar chemical structures, produce what is known as cross-tolerance. This occurs when tolerance to one of the narcotics causes tolerance to others, even if the user has never before used the other drugs. Though it is not exactly known why tolerance develops, it is probably due to a combination of the body more rapidly processing and eliminating the drug and the nervous system "growing used to" the presence of the drug. The latter seems to be the key to the development of tolerance in narcotics users and will be discussed in the next chapter.

Interestingly, an individual does have the capacity to control the development of tolerance to a certain extent. Part of the tolerance to a narcotic seems to be related to the user's expectations prior to taking it. Tolerance, which is also related to how the drug is administered over time, will develop much more quickly in someone who takes a lot of a narcotic in a short period of time than in someone who takes the same amount of the drug over a longer period. Finally, tolerance disappears quickly after drug use is stopped. These three factors, all of which an individual has the potential to control, should always be considered whenever narcotics are being prescribed.

Overdose

Fortunately, as tolerance to opiates increases, so does the lethal dose level, a phenomenon that protects the addict as he or she increases the dosage to produce the desired effect. In fact, without ill effect the typical addict can take doses that would kill the novice user many times over. However, in the case of narcotics, no matter what the experience of the user is, the lethal dose is always dangerously close to the effective dose. As a consequence, many narcotic-related overdoses every year are caused by unknowing individuals who innocently increase their dosages. Though narcotics can cause hypothermia (lower than normal body temperature) and decreased heart rate, leading to cardiac arrest, their principal means of causing a fatal overdose is to depress the respiratory center in the brain. This results in unconsciousness, coma, and death.

The chances of death are even greater when a narcotic is taken along with other central nervous system depressants such as tranquilizers, antihistamines, sedatives, antidepressants, muscle relaxants, anesthetics, and alcohol. Mixing a narcotic with another depressant is extraordinarily risky. This is especially true with the narcotic propoxyphene, which goes under the trade name Darvon. Darvon is a leading cause of those deaths that result from the use of prescription drugs. Most Darvon-related deaths result from combined use with another depressant; many of these deaths are reported as suicides, but about one-third are unintentional.

Operating any kind of heavy or potentially dangerous equipment while using prescription narcotics is extremely hazardous because of the mental confusion and drowsiness that can result from taking the drugs.

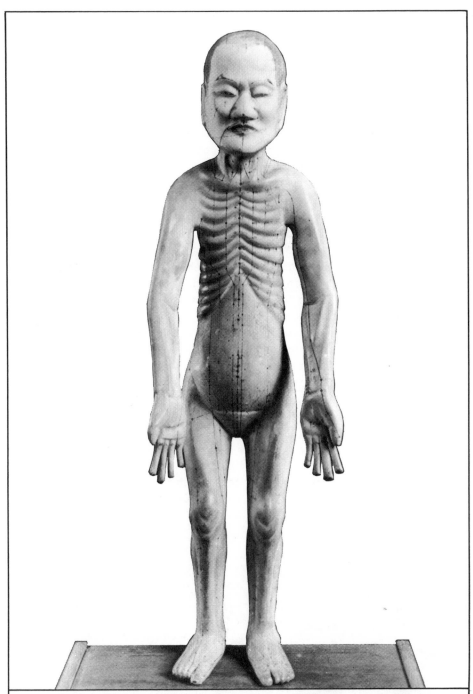

A porcelain model shows points of acupuncture. Still regarded with some skepticism in the Western world, this ancient pain-relieving technique has been used as a surgical anesthetic in China since 1966.

CHAPTER 5

THE ENDOGENOUS OPIATES

Within the past 15 years, our knowledge of pain and analgesia has grown immensely. Fruitful research first began when scientists discovered the powerful analgesic effects of even minute doses of certain synthetic, or laboratory-made, opiate drugs. This convinced researchers that there must be recognition sites, or receptors, in the central nervous system designed specifically for these drugs.

Receptors, which are located on all nerve cells, have the ability to recognize and join with certain neurotransmitters, or message-transmitting chemicals, because of an affinity, or "lock-and-key fit," between the two. Many drugs produce their effects by combining with these receptors and setting off chain reactions that increase the neuron activity. Thus, for morphine to have an effect, it would theoretically have to be attracted to and fit into a certain type of uniquely shaped receptor on the nerve cell.

This theory was first confirmed when the opiate receptors were discovered. By tagging a narcotic with radioactivity (accomplished by attaching radioactive atoms to the narcotic molecule), researchers were able to trace and identify the opiate receptors. Areas with the greatest concentration of opiate receptors are the medial thalamus and the limbic system. The thalamus, a pathway for much of the communication that travels to the higher areas of the brain, can diminish the perception of pain if blocked by a narcotic. Blockade of the limbic system, a center for emotions, inhibits anxiety and other negative emotions associated with pain. Thus, the experimental findings compare well with our knowledge of the opiates' effects.

The opiate receptors are highly selective, accepting only morphine and certain structurally similar compounds, while rejecting even the mirror image of the morphine molecule. When the opiate receptor is occupied by morphine, the neuron undergoes chemical and electrical changes, which lead to the psychological and physiological effects discussed in Chapter 4. Because it *increases* the neuron's natural reactions, morphine is known as an opiate agonist. An opiate antagonist, on the other hand, is a substance that occupies the receptor but does not set off a chemical reaction. Consequently, the antagonists can block the actions of morphine and other agonists. Therefore, use of an antagonist triggers withdrawal in the narcotics addict. The opiate antagonists can also help diagnose narcotics addiction. As will be discussed later, they are also used in the treatment of narcotics addiction.

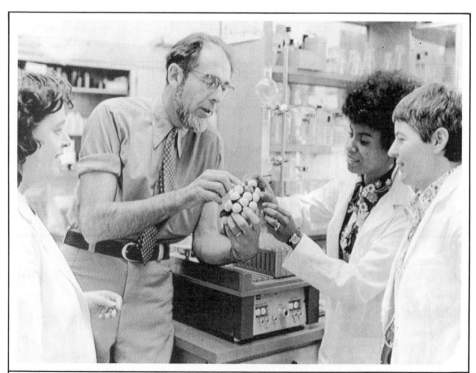

By tagging a narcotic drug with radioactivity, researchers can identify a molecule in brain cells called a "receptor," which, when chemically joined with opiate narcotics, can diminish the perception of pain.

The Discovery of the Endorphins

Realizing the absurdity of the brain having receptors for the molecules of the poppy plant, and harking back to the cases of wounded soldiers being unaware of their injuries, some researchers hypothesized that perhaps the body produces its own, natural analgesics, and that the derivatives of the opium poppy affect us merely because of a similar chemical structure. This hypothesis would help to explain both the analgesic effects of narcotics and the alterations in pain perception brought on by stress, shock, and prior experience.

These researchers were finally rewarded in 1975, when two natural morphine-like peptides were discovered in the pig brain. (Peptides are short chains of amino acids, which are the building blocks of all proteins.) These two peptides produce many of the same effects as narcotics, causing an-

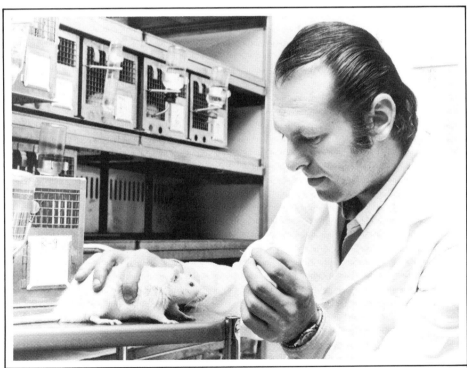

In the mid-1970s scientists discovered a natural morphine-like compound in rats. This finding supported the theory that the human brain generates endorphins, natural analgesics similar in structure to opiates.

algesia, central nervous system depression, and physical dependence. These substances, called *enkephalins* (literally meaning "in the head"), occur predominantly in the brain but also in the intestines, which could perhaps explain the opiates' constipating effects. These two enkephalins, alike in all but the last amino acid in the chain, were named met-enkephalin and leu-enkephalin.

Shortly after the discovery of the enkephalins, a slightly different, larger morphine-like compound was discovered in the rat pituitary. (The pituitary gland produces various hormones that regulate many bodily processes, including growth and reproduction.) This compound was called beta-endorphin, or endogenous morphine. The name *endorphin* has become a generic name for the endogenous opiates and includes a family of related peptides.

The Function of Endorphins in Everyday Life

These relatively recent discoveries shed light on a number of mysterious phenomena. In addition to the fact that shock

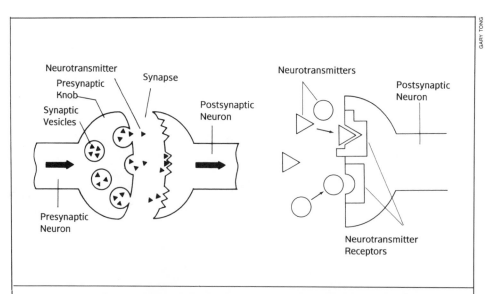

Neurotransmitter activity is illustrated in these two diagrams. The figure on the left shows how one neuron signals another across the synapse by emitting neurotransmitters. The figure on the right shows how each kind of neurotransmitter fits only one kind of receptor on the target neuron.

and stress have analgesic effects, it has long been known that the application of pressure or intense cold upon certain trigger points in the body can inhibit pain. This knowledge is the basis for acupuncture and acupressure. Long treated skeptically by many Westerners, acupuncture now had a possible biological explanation. Perhaps the pressure from the acupuncturist's needle is enough to signal the brain to release its endorphins and block pain. This hypothesis received support from the finding that opiate antagonists (which block the actions of all opiates) eliminate the analgesic effects of acupuncture. Research has also shown that electrical stimulation of certain parts of the brain relieves pain. Once again, because it is known that the opiate antagonists block the release of endorphins, the analgesia caused by brain stimulation may be a result of the release of endorphins from the brain.

Indeed, even the time-honored placebo effect may be a result of endorphin release. The placebo effect is the inhibition of pain by an inactive agent (usually a sugar pill) called a placebo. Placebos have been proven effective in relieving pain an impressive 35% of the time (as compared to 75% for morphine). Many people have explained the placebo as

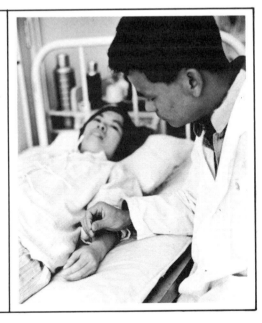

Acupuncture at China's Canton University. By the early 1970s over 400,000 operations using acupuncture anesthesia had been performed in China. Although many Western physicians are dubious about the benefits of acupuncture, the Chinese have used it extensively to treat malaria, stomach problems, rheumatism, arthritis, and to induce sleep.

"working because you think it will work." This explanation, however, does not describe the mechanism by which the placebo works. Recent experiments have shown that the placebo effect is greatest in patients who are under psychological stress and that placebos are more effective on pathological than on experimentally induced pain. These findings parallel the effects of narcotics and imply that the endorphins are at work again. The discovery that the placebo effect can be blocked by the opiate antagonists further suggests that the brain's analgesia system is again working without visible stimulus.

Why Narcotics Work

This basic understanding of the chemistry of the endogenous opiates and their receptors has allowed scientists to clarify their knowledge of narcotics. For example, tolerance and withdrawal, once explained only in broad terms, are now more clearly understood. Previously, scientists could only say

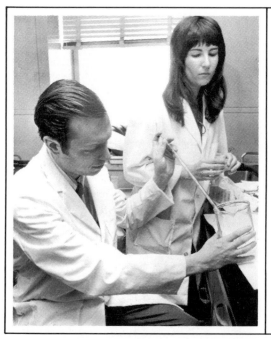

Researchers in pharmacology, the science and study of drugs, have found the greatest concentration of opiate receptors in the thalamus and the limbic system, suggesting that narcotics act primarily on these areas of the brain.

that morphine somehow disrupted the body's delicate balance and that the body then compensated with some adaptive mechanism to restore equilibrium. This was claimed to be the basis for tolerance, because higher amounts of the drug would then be needed to knock the body out of equilibrium. Furthermore, the body depended on the drug to maintain the equilibrium achieved by the adaptive mechanism. Thus, when drug use ceased, the balance would again be disrupted, leading to withdrawal symptoms. Though for a long time this explanation was adequate, it is basically a description that provides little new information. With advances in the study of opiates, scientists can now attempt to explain the addictive aspects of narcotics on a deeper level.

One possible explanation for the development of tolerance is that the neurotransmitters affected by opiates build up during narcotic use and that, consequently, more of the narcotic is needed to block effectively the excess of neurotransmitters. This neurotransmitter buildup would also explain withdrawal, as the abrupt cessation of drug use would allow the excess neurotransmitters to pass across the synapse, overwhelming the receptors and shattering the body's equilibrium.

Another possibility is that narcotics exert their effect by decreasing the production of an enzyme within the neuron. (Enzymes are agents that promote the chemical reactions within the cell.) When the enzyme level is decreased, a feedback mechanism within the cell alerts the neuron's enzyme-manufacturing components that there is a shortage, and these components subsequently step up production. Tolerance to a narcotic is said to have developed when the neuron produces a sufficient amount of enzymes even in the presence of the repressing opiate. At about this point, withdrawal of the narcotic will take away the inhibition, causing enzyme production to rise above the normal amount and disrupt the body's equilibrium. This sends the addict into withdrawal. Withdrawal will continue until the feedback mechanism senses an enzyme surplus and causes production to decrease again.

Finally, recent research has indicated an important role for the noradrenergic system in the effects of narcotics. This research indicated that the noradrenergic system, which plays a role in the production of anxiety among other things, is inhibited by the opiates. Sometimes, inhibition of a chemical "sending" system in the brain causes an increase in the sensitivity of the "receiving" system (i.e. the receptors for that chemical). There is in fact evidence that the opiates cause increased sensitivity of the noradrenergic receptors. This increasing sensitivity means that the user must take higher and higher narcotic doses just to maintain equilibrium (this is tolerance). This hypersensitivity of the receiving system would also cause powerful negative effects, such as increased anxiety, once the opiates are no longer around to inhibit the sending system (this is withdrawal). Scientists have bolstered this theory by showing that noradrenaline levels in the brain change with narcotic withdrawal. They have also shown that drugs that inhibit the noradrenergic system can reduce the signs of narcotic withdrawal. This last finding is important because of its practical implications—the addict can more easily give up drugs if withdrawal is made a little more bearable.

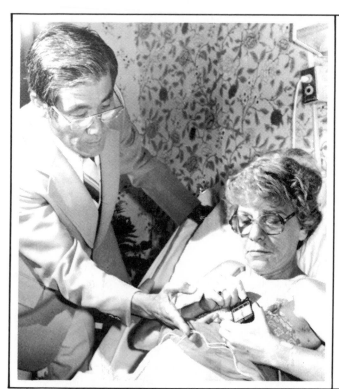

A doctor shows a patient how to operate an electrical painkilling device, which reduces the need for prescription pain relievers. Researchers are continually searching for alternatives to prescription narcotics because of the potential for dependence and abuse inherent in the drugs.

A final theory on narcotics dependence claims that tolerance occurs because the opiate receptors' feedback mechanisms, upon sensing the presence of opiates, decrease endorphin production and thus necessitate an increase in drug dosage. This increase keeps the body at equilibrium. But once drug use is stopped, the receptors are open again— as the narcotics have basically taken over the endorphins' job—and the pain pathways are uninhibited, bringing on withdrawal. Addiction has thus set in, as the user feels compelled to keep the receptors full but can only do so by artificial means.

With this last theory in mind, researchers have recently been looking for some difference in the endorphin levels of addicts. Researchers suspect that these individuals become dependent on narcotics because of some endogenous-opiate deficiency. Success in this area of study may allow us to diagnose those individuals who are at a higher risk for addiction.

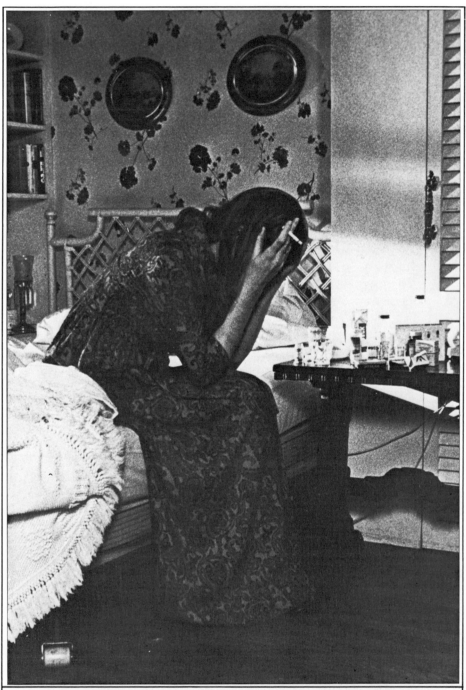

Withdrawal from prescription narcotics is a long and painful ordeal. Symptoms include anxiety, insomnia, fever, nausea, increased pulse rate and blood pressure, and muscle spasms.

CHAPTER 6

PRESCRIPTIONS FOR NARCOTICS

*N*arcotics, like all drugs, are ranked on a scale from Schedule I to Schedule V, according to the U.S. Controlled Substances Act of 1970. A drug's ranking describes its level of usefulness and risk for abuse. For example, heroin is classified as a Schedule I drug, meaning that it has no medicinal uses and is highly abusable. As the classification rises to Schedule V, the drugs become increasingly safer and have proven medical value. For the most part, the prescription narcotics fall within Schedule II and Schedule III, meaning that they have medicinal uses but also a relatively high abuse potential.

Narcotics are prescribed as cough suppressants and antidiarrheals, and as analgesics for moderate and severe pain. The types of pain that usually require a narcotic include pain associated with fractures and other traumas, angina pectoris (severe pain and constriction of the heart), kidney stones and gallstones, acute myocardial infarction (lack of blood to part of the heart, resulting in shock, cardiac failure, pain similar to that caused by angina, and even sudden death), and terminal cancer. In addition, narcotics are used to ease the pain of childbirth and are often administered to supplement the analgesic, anti-anxiety, and sedative effects of anesthetics prior to surgery.

The primary risk involved with narcotics use is addiction. Because of their addictive potential, narcotics should not be used for pain that can be relieved by one of the milder analgesics such as aspirin. However, a doctor will usually not hesitate to prescribe narcotics for short-term therapy if the non-narcotic analgesics are insufficient. On the other hand, if the pain is long-lasting, narcotics are much less advisable and are consequently less likely to be prescribed because of the increased risk of addiction. If the milder analgesics are insufficient for chronic pain, a narcotic with low addictive potential and long duration of effect will often be prescribed (a drug with long duration of effect does not need to be taken as often, which reduces the risk of addiction). But even this is risky, as dependence can still result and is often as debilitating as the pain itself. Thus, if the pain reaches this point, other methods of control, such as neurosurgery, are sometimes tried.

Overdosing on narcotics is a great risk because of the small difference between effective and lethal doses. The level of danger rises even more when the narcotics are taken in combination with other depressants. In addition, very young and very old people are at a special risk of narcotics-induced respiratory depression. Obviously, narcotics are also dangerous for persons with asthma or other respiratory impairments.

Opiates should also be used with caution by pregnant women, because these drugs cross the placental barrier and enter the fetus. Thus, addicted mothers have been known to give birth to addicted infants. Even mothers who have received a narcotic merely to ease the pain of labor have given birth to babies suffering from severe respiratory depression. Finally, many narcotics are excreted in the mother's breast milk. There are documented cases of breast-fed babies who have become addicted to these drugs, especially in cases in which the mother is using methadone to overcome her heroin addiction.

Others at special risk from using prescription narcotics include alcoholics; former drug addicts; people with head injuries (because narcotics increase pressure in the brain), hypothyroidism (insufficient thyroid secretion), and liver damage; and emotionally unstable or suicidal individuals (narcotics aggravate these emotional problems). People without these conditions should nevertheless be careful when using narcotics, as their effects can be greatly influenced by such common factors as body weight and time of day of administration. The user should always remember that drugs affect people differently and that individual differences can overrule a drug's normal effect.

A person who is taking a prescription narcotic should also take other precautions. Driving and working with dangerous machinery should be avoided whenever possible. Narcotics create a false sense of well-being that masks potentially dangerous coordination deficits. Also, rising from a sitting or lying position should be done with care, as this may aggravate the nausea, dizziness, and vomiting that are sometimes associated with narcotics use. Finally, after a long period of narcotics use, one should not abruptly stop administration without first consulting a physician, since severe withdrawal effects may result.

Opiate Agonists

Opiate agonists are those drugs that bind with opiate receptors and thereby produce their characteristic effects.

Opium, once as common as aspirin, is rarely used today. The extraction of morphine and the development of synthetic

According to the Pharmaceutical Manufacturers Association, the United States is the leading developer of pharmaceutical drugs—an achievement due in part to the protection U.S. patent laws offer researchers.

narcotics have rendered opium somewhat obsolete. Thera-peutically, it is considered an old-fashioned remedy, although it is still used occasionally for the relief of severe pain. Some-times it is given as a rectal suppository for the relief of ure-thral-spasm pain. Opium is also used to treat infants who are born addicted because of their mothers' abuse of narcotics. In these cases, it is usually given in the form of paregoric, a mixture of opium, camphor, benzoic acid, and alcohol. Opi-um's principal use, however, is as an antidiarrheal, although tolerance develops to this effect.

UPI/BETTMANN ARCHIVE

In Harlem, an area of New York City, "Mother" Clara Hale is shown with some of the homeless small children she cares for who were born addicted to heroin and crack cocaine. Because narcotics can affect the fetus, pregnant women who abuse these drugs risk giving birth to addicted infants. In addition, both mothers and babies are at risk for developing the fatal disease AIDS if the drugs are administered intravenously.

Opium is classified as a Schedule II or Schedule III drug, depending on its form, and is abused because of the sedation and euphoria that closely follow the initially unpleasant effects such as nausea and vomiting. On the street, opium is known as o, op, tar, black pills, black stuff, brown stuff, canned stuff, mash Allah, gum, and hop. Sometimes a heroin addict will abuse paregoric if no heroin is available. Taken orally, about one quart of this mixture is necessary to bring about the desired effects. To decrease the necessary dosage and to achieve an added rush, paregoric is sometimes injected intravenously, though this usually has damaging effects on the veins. For an even greater high, paregoric is also sometimes added to antihistamines and injected. This potent concoction, known as "Blue Velvet," is no longer popular because it sometimes causes plugged veins and death. Another problem connected with the use of opium is its tendency to mask and even aggravate dehydration in the user. This can make the drug's effects inconsistent, especially in the young user.

A New York City opium den in 1926. The introduction of opium smoking to the West in the mid-1800s coincided with the immigration of thousands of Chinese laborers. A subculture of addicts eventually developed.

Morphine In 1813 morphine became the first pure opiate chemical to be isolated from opium. Morphine is also the main narcotic chemical in opium, making up 10% of the weight of raw opium. Because for a number of years it was the only pure opiate chemical, and because it was so much stronger than opium itself, morphine became widely used and abused by the 20th century. It was the primary narcotic used in the Civil War and the main drug included in patent medicines.

Morphine is considered a strong analgesic and is used (primarily by injection) for both severe acute and severe chronic pain. Morphine is also used to supplement anesthesia prior to operations and to ease the pain of childbirth. The drug is sometimes given to alleviate some of the symptoms associated with pulmonary edema (swelling of the lungs) and is the drug of choice for treating heart attack victims. Because of its powerful cough-suppressant properties, morphine is also a good analgesic to use for pain that results from a cough.

Morphine quickly causes psychological dependence, followed by physical dependence. However, it is no longer the major drug of abuse because addicts now prefer the stronger, shorter-acting heroin or cocaine. On the streets, morphine

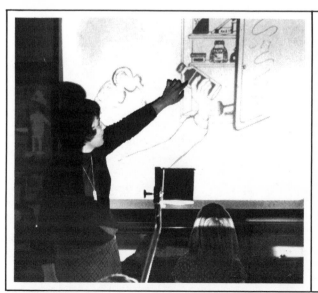

A kindergarten teacher explains the danger of drugs commonly found in the family medicine cabinet. Educators hope that providing young people with information regarding the hazards of drugs will reduce the chances of accidental misuse and overdose and discourage them from experimenting with potentially addictive narcotics.

is called m, morph, morphy, dreamer, M.S., Miss Emma, Miss Morph, birdie powder, big M., first line, gunk, hocus, Mary, white stuff, and God's medicine.

Codeine is another naturally occurring constituent of opium, though it can also be synthesized from morphine. It is used to treat mild to moderate pain, including menstrual pain, and as an antidiarrheal. Its primary use is as a cough suppressant. Codeine is often combined with aspirin to increase aspirin's analgesic effectiveness. It is also sometimes mixed with phenacetin (a painkiller), caffeine, and aspirin, though some experts question whether this preparation is any more effective than the codeine-aspirin combination.

Codeine's effects usually set in after 15 to 30 minutes and last for 4 to 6 hours. Though these effects are less intense

A student pharmacist at the Los Angeles Free Clinic. Narcotics, which are most commonly prescribed as cough suppressants, antidiarrheals, and painkillers, are also used to ease the pain of childbirth.

than morphine's, the respiratory depression induced by codeine is roughly equal to that of morphine. Paradoxically, the ingestion of a high dose of codeine can cause excitement. Also, research has shown that high doses of codeine cause abnormal development in rats, though it is not yet known if similar effects are produced in humans.

Though in some forms it is a Schedule II drug and psychological dependence on it can develop fairly rapidly, codeine is not a major drug of abuse. In fact, because of its weak effects (it is roughly 10% as potent as morphine), codeine is the opiate agonist with perhaps the lowest potential for abuse and is therefore seldom used on the street. However, on occasion it is seen in the street and in these cases it is called "pops" or "schoolboy." Codeine can also be mixed with a sedative to form the potent "4s and Dors" ("4s" for Tylenol with codeine-4, and "Dors" for Doriden, the sedative). Finally, codeine is sometimes abused in the form of cough medicines.

Propoxyphene is generally used for mild to moderate pain and has little or no cough-suppressant properties. It is less potent than codeine, and some authorities question whether it is even as effective as aspirin. However, propoxyphene is one of the primary narcotics of abuse and among this class of drugs it is the leading cause of death. Introduced to the United States as Darvon in 1957, propoxyphene has been a best-seller among prescription painkillers, with an estimated 20 million pills being sold annually. Though generally safe when used as directed, Darvon becomes a killer if used improperly. The gap between the effective and lethal doses of Darvon is low, and therefore slight dose increases can be dangerous. In fact, doses only slightly higher than those that are recommended have been fatal. The danger is heightened by the fact that the recreational user needs large doses of the drug to produce a high.

As with other narcotics, it is dangerous to mix Darvon with other depressants. Although propoxyphene-related overdoses have declined in recent years, the drug is still one of the leading causes of death among prescription drugs. In 1988 the Drug Abuse Warning Network (DAWN) reported 271 deaths nationwide from its use. (See Appendix III.) A majority of these deaths are probable suicides, but as many as one-third may be the result of accidental misuse.

Because of these overdose statistics, propoxyphene was placed in Schedule IV by the Controlled Substances Act of 1970. This ranking limits prescription refills to five times every six months. Furthermore, pharmacists are required to keep special records of all such prescriptions. Unfortunately, Schedule IV ranking puts no limits on drug production, and prescriptions can still be filled by phone. Consequently, many experts want propoxyphene to be placed on the stricter Schedule II. This would automatically limit the drug's manufacture, ban refills, and prohibit filled-by-phone prescriptions. In 1978 Dr. Sidney Wolfe, head of a Washington, D.C., health research group, asked for a ban on Darvon, calling it the "deadliest prescription drug in the U.S." The Department

A pharmacy in the 1950s. Introduced to the United States in 1957, Darvon (propoxyphene) is a popular prescription narcotic. However, it is also extremely hazardous and sometimes lethal if abused.

of Health, Education, and Welfare turned down the proposal. However, the Food and Drug Administration (FDA), aware of the problems of overdose and addiction (it takes only 8 to 12 pills of Darvon per day to cause addiction), distributed special advisories on the dangers associated with propoxyphene to doctors and pharmacists nationwide. Then, in 1980, the FDA requested physicians to write "no refills" on prescriptions for those on short-term therapy, and later asked that all prescriptions be written out rather than phoned in.

On the street, propoxyphene comes in tablets and capsules called "pinks" or "red and grays." It can be found alone in Darvon and Darvon-N; in combination with aspirin in Darvon with ASA, and in Darvon-N with ASA; with acetaminophen (a painkiller) in Darvocet, Darvocet-N 100, Wygesic, and SK-65 APAP; and with aspirin/phenacetin/caffeine combinations (known as A.P.C.) in Darvon Compound, Darvon Compound 65, and SK-65 Compound. Problems can be caused by the inclusion of aspirin and acetaminophen in these pills. The addition of caffeine can cause insomnia and anxiety in

In 1978, five years after Senator Gaylord Nelson (pictured) called for a restriction on the promotion of prescription drugs like Darvon, Dr. Sidney Wolfe, head of a Washington, D.C., health research group, proposed a ban on Darvon, which was widely abused. The Food and Drug Administration (FDA) rejected the ban, but did issue warnings about the drug's effects, and it placed stricter regulations on prescriptions.

the user, which may lead to a desire for tranquilizers and other such drugs with abuse potential.

Methadone was first synthesized by German chemists during World War II and used as an analgesic. Today it is frequently used to alleviate pain in terminally ill cancer patients, but since the late 1960s its major use has been for the treatment of heroin addicts. Methadone's many possible applications have led to widespread illicit use and abuse. In fact, according to recent DAWN data (see Appendixes II and III), methadone accounts for more drug-related deaths and emergency-room admissions than propoxyphene, although methadone itself is outranked by heroin, currently the number-3 killer drug (cocaine is number 1, followed by alcohol used in combination with other drugs). Despite its potential for abuse, however, methadone has become the focus of renewed interest as an alternative to heroin in an effort to combat AIDS. By administering methadone in drinkable form to heroin addicts, health authorities hope to decrease illicit intravenous drug use, a major means of spreading the AIDS virus.

Methadone is dissimilar to morphine in chemical structure but has comparable analgesic action and similar side effects. Orally, it is better absorbed than morphine, and its analgesic effects are longer lasting. Also, methadone produces less sedation and euphoria than morphine.

Besides being used in detoxification and maintenance, methadone can be used to reduce severe pain. It is especially useful for severe chronic pain because of its long-lasting analgesic action. Though the effects of the first doses only last for 4 to 6 hours, with repeated administration the analgesic effects can last from 22 to 48 hours. This extended duration means fewer administrations, which, in turn, mean lower chances of dependence. Methadone has a good antitussive action but is no longer used as a cough suppressant. However, it is often used in cases of severe pain that is accompanied by a cough.

Methadone comes in solutions, injectables, and tablets. For use in maintenance, methadone is usually dissolved in fruit juices. In tablet form, methadone is called Dolophine. There are certain risks involved in the use of methadone. When high doses are ingested, the drug can induce convulsions. Methadone can also cause problems for pregnant women who are undergoing methadone maintenance. Their babies often have lowered birth weights and sometimes experience withdrawal. Furthermore, there appears to be a higher rate of sudden infant death syndrome (SIDS) among these babies. Methadone can also show up in the mother's breast milk if she is on maintenance.

Finally, a special danger associated with the use of methadone arises when the drug abuser, in search of a better high, attempts to inject a solution made from a methadone tablet. To discourage injection, tablet manufacturers include inert ingredients in the pills. When they are dissolved in a solution and injected, these ingredients can lodge in the lungs and cause serious lung conditions and even death.

Cherry-flavored methadone is dispensed in small cups for heroin addicts at a Baltimore clinic. Frequently used in heroin-free maintenance programs, methadone is dissolved in fruit juice and consumed orally. This method of ingestion causes little sedation or euphoria and eliminates the ritual of the needle associated with the injection of heroin; it also decreases the spread of infectious diseases like AIDS associated with intravenous drug use.

Meperidine was introduced in 1939 as a means of reducing the pain associated with muscle spasms. It was later discovered that the drug had many other remarkable analgesic abilities, and it soon became the second leading painkiller (after morphine). Today meperidine is commonly abused by doctors and is regularly overprescribed for patients, usually in the mistaken belief that it has little potential for addiction. It comes in solutions and injections under the name Demerol, and is available in capsules and tablets as well.

Only about one-tenth as potent as morphine, meperidine is still a fairly strong analgesic and is used for treatment of moderate to severe pain. Meperidine is also used to supplement anesthesia before an operation and to relieve the pain of labor during childbirth. This drug has a rapid onset and a short duration of effect, peaking within an hour and lasting for only 2 to 4 hours. This makes it a valuable drug for the relief of short-term pain. Meperidine has the advantages over morphine of a shorter period of respiratory depression, fewer peripheral effects, and less of a constipating effect. On the other hand, tolerance to many of the effects of meperidine grows quickly, and the short duration of effect necessitates many administrations, which can facilitate the development of addiction. The drug has little antitussive or antidiarrheal actions.

As for adverse effects, meperidine can cause problems when given to women in labor, often making breathing difficult despite its weak effect on respiration. Furthermore, large doses of meperidine can cause twitches, tremors, and convulsions. The drug is especially dangerous when mixed with MAO inhibitors, a class of antidepressant. If taken within two weeks of using a MAO inhibitor, meperidine can cause symptoms similar to those seen in acute narcotic overdose, including convulsions, hypertension (a condition characterized by high blood pressure), coma, and even death.

Oxycodone, a morphine derivative, is often used when aspirin is no longer effective. With an analgesic effect that peaks within an hour, oxycodone is used mainly for short-term rather than chronic pain. This drug's analgesic effect is roughly equal to that of morphine, and it is used in cases of moderate to moderately severe pain such as that experienced with dislocations, injuries, simple fractures, neuralgia, and bursitis.

Like many of the prescription narcotics, oxycodone comes in a solution or as a tablet or capsule. It is also included in the tablets Percodan, Percodan-Demi, and Percocet-5. Although it has fewer negative side effects than morphine, oxycodone induces the same level of dependence.

Oxymorphone is another morphine derivative and a Schedule II drug. It has greater analgesic action and less of a constipating effect than morphine. However, its other side effects, such as nausea and vomiting, are more severe than those of morphine. This drug has little antitussive action and is used primarily to relieve anxiety and pain associated with pulmonary edema. Sold as Numorphan, oxymorphone is also used postoperatively for sedation and analgesia.

Levorphanol is a synthetic narcotic that is equal to or greater than morphine in its analgesic effects. A Schedule II drug that causes both tolerance and dependence, levorphanol nonetheless has a low incidence of abuse. When compared to morphine, levorphanol, like methadone, is better absorbed when ingested orally and has a longer duration of effect (about 6 to 8 hours). Levorphanol also causes less nausea, vomiting, and constipation than morphine, though it causes

NOTICE
As of September 1, 1973
NEEDLES and SYRINGES
will require
Doctors Prescription

By requiring a doctor's prescription for needles and syringes, authorities intended to hinder the street abuse of methadone, which in 1973 was responsible for more deaths in New York City than heroin.

greater sedation and muscle stimulation, both of which are undesirable.

Levorphanol, which is sold in tablets as Levo-Dromeran, is used to supplement anesthesia and to treat moderate to severe pain such as that associated with trauma, cancers, tumors, myocardial infarction, and renal and biliary colic.

Hydrocodone is one of the primary antitussives among the narcotics. Similar to, but more potent than, codeine, this drug is also used for the relief of moderate pain. Hydrocodone has an addictive potential that is lower than that of morphine but higher than that of codeine. Hydrocodone withdrawal is milder than that of morphine, and it usually takes a few weeks of use before any dependence is evident. This narcotic is sold in tablets as Tussionex, Vicodin, and Duradyne DHC.

Hydromorphone is another narcotic antitussive with strong analgesic qualities. It is more potent than morphine while having fewer adverse side effects. Hydromorphone is

Strips of aspirin tablets in tamper-resistant packaging. Codeine, about 10% as potent as morphine and with one of the lowest abuse potentials among the opiate narcotics, is frequently used in cough medicines or mixed with aspirin to enhance the latter's painkilling effects.

used to treat severe pain, especially in cancer patients. Its trade names are Hydromorphone HCL and Dilaudid.

Opiate Agonist-Antagonists

The opiate agonist-antagonists, or partial agonists, combine the activity of the opiate agonists with the receptor-blocking activity of the antagonists. The partial agonists have many of the effects of the "pure" agonists, including analgesia, respiratory depression, drowsiness, sedation, and pupillary constriction. But the partial agonists differ from the agonists in that they often produce an uneasy state of dysphoria marked by tiredness, disorientation, feelings of drunkenness, and even hallucinations. However, most of the partial agonists have milder effects than the agonists. Moreover, the level of dysphoria experienced is usually dose-dependent. Therapeutic doses often have little adverse effect, whereas higher doses may induce a whole range of ill effects.

The partial agonists, first synthesized in 1954, are currently popular because they are less addictive than the pure agonists. Furthermore, when the dose level of these drugs is increased, their respiratory-depressive actions do not rise significantly. Their low addiction potential is attributable to their adverse side effects and general lack of ability to produce euphoria.

Pentazocine is an agonist with some weak antagonist activity. It is one-half to one-sixth as potent as morphine. This makes it effective enough to block moderate to severe pain. It also has a dependence potential lower than that of propoxyphene or codeine. Pentazocine produces adverse effects that are roughly comparable to those of morphine, though it causes less vomiting and more sedation, nausea, euphoria, and dizziness. Pentazocine can also cause headaches, insomnia, weakness, and mood alterations, as well as occasional confusion, disorientation, and even hallucinations.

Although it is a partial agonist, pentazocine still has a high abuse rate. This is because narcotics addicts often extract the active drug from the tablet it comes in, mix it with an antihistamine, and inject it intravenously. On the street, this potent combination is known as "Ts and Blues." Recognizing this abuse, the manufacturers of the pentazocine tablet have recently added the narcotic antagonist naloxone to the tablet. This eliminates the high associated with the drug without affecting its analgesic potency. However, oral abuse of these tablets still occurs.

The effects of pentazocine peak between the first and third hour after administration and can last for three hours or more. Sold in tablets under the trade names Talacen and Talwin, the drug is used in hospitals for pre-operative analgesia and sedation. Its effects are comparable to those of morphine and meperidine. Pentazocine is not recommended for treating the pain associated with heart attacks because it makes the heart work harder. Also, use of this drug by an addict currently taking narcotics is inadvisable, as its antagonist activity may induce withdrawal. Special caution should also be taken when the patient has a head injury or if his or her mental stability is in question, since these conditions can be aggravated by taking pentazocine.

Butorphanol is a partial agonist that, on a weight basis, is 4 to 7 times as potent as morphine. It also has antagonistic actions that are 30 times those of pentazocine. Butorphanol

At the Indiana University School of Medicine in Indianapolis, a doctor examines devices used for drug testing of participants in the 1987 Pan American Games held in that city. Drug use among athletes has caused increasing concern in recent years, and many sports competitions limit participation to those who test drug-free.

UPI/BETTMANN ARCHIVE

produces a relatively high degree of sedation, but it causes less respiratory depression than morphine and has antitussive properties as well. Butorphanol has a low abuse potential. Nevertheless, care must be taken that the drug is not administered merely in anticipation of pain, for this has led to unnecessary addiction. Butorphanol does have a number of adverse side effects such as nausea, dizziness, clamminess, lethargy, and confusion, as well as hallucinations, vomiting, constipation, cramps, rashes, and unusual dreams.

Butorphanol takes effect within 1 hour of administration and lasts for 3 to 4 hours. It is used to alleviate the moderate to severe pain associated with both acute and chronic conditions. It has proven helpful as an analgesic during surgery and in treating cancer, neuropathic problems, burns, orthopedic problems, and renal colic. The drug is also used pre-operatively with anesthesia and is considered safe for use during pregnancy and childbirth.

Butorphanol comes in injectable form as Stadol and is associated with certain risks. For instance, like pentazocine, butorphanol should be used with care by the addict, as its antagonist properties can trigger withdrawal. Butorphanol can also be dangerous to people with certain heart conditions, as it increases the work of the heart. As with many

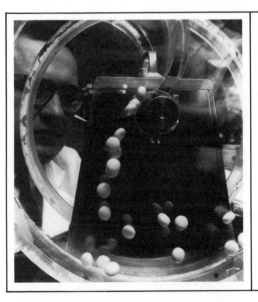

Some pharmaceutical companies employ a "friabilator," an apparatus that bounces tablets around to determine their resistance to any damage that might occur in manufacture, packaging, and shipping.

other narcotics, driving and working with dangerous equipment while under the influence of this drug is risky.

Nalbuphine is a partial agonist related to naloxone and oxymorphone. It has 10 times the antagonist action of pentazocine but has analgesic and respiratory effects roughly equal to those of morphine. Its side effects are similar to those of morphine. Sedation is common, and sweatiness, clamminess, vomiting, cramps, and headaches can also occur. Being a partial agonist, however, nalbuphine has a low abuse potential (about equal to that of pentazocine). Furthermore, unlike some of the other partial agonists, nalbuphine has no adverse cardiac effects.

Nalbuphine takes effect quickly (within 15 minutes) but lasts a relatively long time (from 3 to 6 hours). The drug is usually given to reduce moderate to severe pain, such as that associated with cancer, surgery, childbirth, orthopedic problems, and migraine or vascular headaches.

Nalbuphine comes in an injectable form called Nubain. Nubain does not normally precipitate withdrawal in the narcotics addict, but it can do so in high doses and thus is usually not used to treat addicts unless they are off drugs. Also, nalbuphine can itself cause withdrawal when its use is stopped. The safety of the use of nalbuphine by children or during pregnancy has not been established. But when used to ease the pain of childbirth, this drug can cause respiratory depression in the infant.

Staff counselors meet informally at a New York drug rehabilitation center. In "rehab," addicts receive psychological as well as pharmacological treatment as they try to overcome their drug habits.

CHAPTER 7

THE TREATMENT OF NARCOTICS ADDICTION

Narcotics addiction is treated in a number of ways. The three main forms of treatment are psychological therapy, pharmacological treatment, and enforced treatment.

Psychological Therapy

Though psychological principles are inherent in almost every form of treatment, psychotherapy alone is generally unsuccessful in treating drug addiction. In fact, one study found it successful only 2% of the time. However, psychotherapy can be helpful if it is used in conjunction with one of the other forms of treatment, as it can help combat the negative feelings and low self-esteem commonly seen in the addict.

Pharmacological Treatment

Methadone Maintenance Pharmacological treatment has a better track record than psychological therapy in treating narcotics dependence. Perhaps the primary form of this kind of treatment is methadone maintenance. In 1990 an estimated 100,000 people were undergoing this treatment. In a methadone maintenance program the addict is helped off the narcotic that he or she is abusing by being switched to the opiate methadone. Methadone, a long-lasting, mild narcotic, does not greatly interfere with everyday life and is thus seen as a "lesser evil" than the narcotic it replaces. Taken orally, methadone causes very little apathy or sedation and has almost no euphoric action. In fact, because of cross-tolerance, methadone can prevent the euphoric effects of other narcotics and thus help to keep the addict from returning to the original drug of abuse. Furthermore, the use of oral methadone eliminates the entire ritual surrounding the injection of the drug, which is often seen as a powerful reinforcer of the addict's behavior; it also decreases the risk of contracting AIDS and other infectious diseases, as noted earlier.

During the typical methadone maintenance program, the patient is initially given methadone 6 times a week at a clinic and once a week for take-home administration. After three months of this regimen, the patient is allowed to take home up to 4 doses a week (though never more than 2 doses at a time) if certain conditions have been met, such as proven responsibility, a record of employment, and suitable progress

A cartoon depicting the conflict between the two main therapies used in treating drug abuse: the medicine man, representing chemotherapy and pharmacological (drug) treatment, and the emotional healer, representing psychotherapy. In the case of treating narcotics dependence, pharmacological treatment programs such as methadone maintenance have proved far more successful than psychotherapy.

in other areas. After two years of treatment, the patient is usually only required to come in to the clinic twice a week.

The idea behind methadone maintenance is that the addict has gone through basically irreversible metabolic changes and that methadone preserves the addict's equilibrium while representing an improvement over the original habit. Methadone's long-lasting nature also provides for a more consistent level of the drug in the blood. This eliminates the extreme effects produced by some of the other narcotics. In addition, methadone maintenance keeps the addict in close touch with a clinic. Most important, however, is the fact that addicts usually prefer methadone maintenance over other forms of treatment and consequently are more cooperative. This probably contributes to the 80% success rate that the methadone maintenance program showed in a five-year study conducted in the 1960s.

Nurse giving addicted patients their daily dose of methadone mixed with Tang at a San Francisco methadone clinic. In 1990, an estimated 100,000 people were undergoing methadone treatment for heroin withdrawal.

The main problem with methadone maintenance is that the patient is merely switching drugs. He or she still is very much an addict. Although addiction to methadone may be somewhat more socially acceptable than addiction to heroin, any addiction is undesirable. And, unfortunately, in some cities methadone addiction is growing to levels that surpass even heroin addiction. Another problem with the methadone maintenance program is that the patient is allowed to leave the clinic with varying amounts of the drug for take-home administration. Though take-home doses are only given on certain conditions and after a certain level of trust is assumed, the potential for abuse still remains. In an attempt to achieve an extra rush, some patients try to inject their take-home doses intravenously. This can result in methadone overdose, which, like any narcotic overdose, can end in death. The many methadone overdoses every year serve as a grim and ironic reminder of the dangers of take-home administration. Further problems can arise when the take-home doses fall into the wrong hands. Children die every year after drinking methadone/fruit-juice mixtures that they find in the refrigerator and innocently think are plain orange juice.

LAAM, a newer drug, does not present some of the problems associated with methadone maintenance. LAAM is similar to methadone in effects, side effects, and withdrawal, and is used in the same manner in maintenance programs. But LAAM has a significantly longer duration of effect than methadone, lasting up to three days. This means fewer administrations, causing less interference in the patient's life, and fewer take-home administrations, thus decreasing the potential for abuse.

Opiate Antagonists A less common type of pharmacological treatment of addiction is the use of opiate antagonists, or drugs that specifically inhibit the opiates' effect on the brain. The opiate antagonists, such as naloxone, are nonaddictive, have no abuse potential, and prevent the euphoric effects of the other narcotics. Hence, when these drugs are taken, the narcotic no longer produces the effects that had previously reinforced the addict's abusive behavior.

Unfortunately, the antagonists also precipitate withdrawal in the patient who is still under the influence of opiates. Thus, they should be given only to addicts who have already been through withdrawal. This prevents some patients from even getting started on this treatment. Furthermore, patients do not always comply with antagonist treatment, preferring their narcotics to the noxious-tasting antagonists, which also have unpleasant side effects such as irritability, motor incoordination, and hallucinations. Because the antagonists, unlike methadone, are nonaddicting, the patient does not feel compelled to take them and can easily drop out of the treatment program. The antagonists do not even quell the addict's craving for a narcotics fix. A final problem with this form of treatment is the short duration of the antagonist's effects (3 to 4 hours). This necessitates up

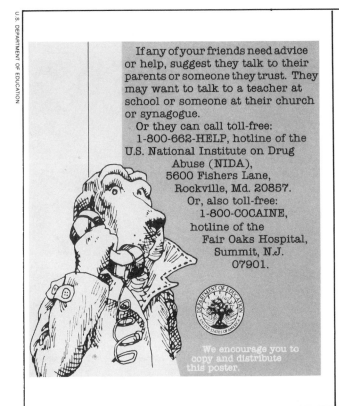

If any of your friends need advice or help, suggest they talk to their parents or someone they trust. They may want to talk to a teacher at school or someone at their church or synagogue.

Or they can call toll-free: 1-800-662-HELP, hotline of the U.S. National Institute on Drug Abuse (NIDA), 5600 Fishers Lane, Rockville, Md. 20857. Or, also toll-free: 1-800-COCAINE, hotline of the Fair Oaks Hospital, Summit, N.J. 07901.

We encourage you to copy and distribute this poster.

A poster aimed at young people offers suggestions for drug-related advice and help, including two hotline numbers. In addition to providing emotional support for the often desperate caller, drug hotlines can refer the person to available drug services and treatment centers.

to 6 administrations per day. Nonetheless, many people champion this type of treatment because, when it is successful, it represents the defeat of addiction, as opposed to the continued addiction seen in methadone maintenance.

The STEPS Method Another pharmacological treatment for addiction is known as the STEPS method. The philosophy behind STEPS is similar to that behind methadone maintenance. The addict's habit is replaced by a safer addiction in a better environment. Unlike the maintenance method, however, the STEPS method works to decrease the degree of dependence in a number of steps until the addict is taken off drugs completely.

In the typical STEPS procedure, the addict's drug (usually heroin) is replaced by an intravenous injection of morphine three times daily. Although the addict is ingesting a lot of drugs and is experiencing a significant high, he or she is at

A math class at a rehabilitation center provides educational services and basic living needs for recovering drug addicts.

least doing so under safe, sterile conditions. After a suitable period of time, the addict is graduated to subcutaneous injections (injections just beneath the skin) of morphine. Subcutaneous injection gives less of a high but is enough to keep the addict satisfied. At the appropriate time, morphine is replaced by daily methadone administration, which is eventually replaced by LAAM. With each of these steps, the high that the addict receives is less intense and occurs less frequently. The next step is the replacement of LAAM by an opiate antagonist, usually naltrexone. With this step, the addict is basically put on antagonist treatment. Finally, the antagonist treatment is replaced by total abstinence. Thus, this program, which takes one to five years to complete, ideally accomplishes something that methadone maintenance programs cannot—it gets the addict off drugs completely.

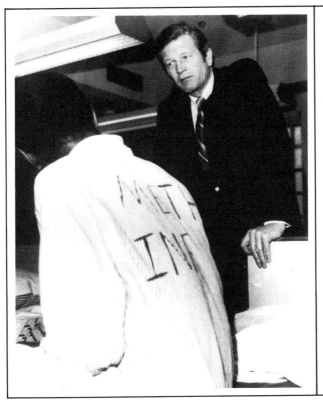

Former New York City Mayor John Lindsay speaks with an inmate in a methadone maintenance program at Manhattan's Tombs prison. Despite the success rate of methadone treatments, critics point out that such care simply involves replacing one addiction with another.

Clonidine as said in Chapter 4, the noradrenergic system seems to play a role in the effects of narcotics. There is now evidence that blocking hyperactivity of this system during withdrawal can reduce many of the negative effects normally seen. Clonidine reduces activity in the noradrenergic system and has been shown to reduce signs of withdrawal in the addict, thus facilitating the process.

Enforced Treatment

The third type of treatment for narcotics addiction is enforced treatment. This can include any of the previously discussed treatments in conjunction with some form of strict control, or *rational authority* treatment. One such form is

Although rock music has been frequently associated with drugs, concerts such as this one in New York City have tried to discourage young people from chemical abuse by alerting them to its dangers and emphasizing the positive quality of life without drugs.

the communal home method. This usually consists of the addict moving into a home with other addicts, giving up narcotics "cold turkey," and being confronted by ex-addicts. These confrontations, which consist of scolding and ridiculing the addict's lifestyle, are complemented by group therapy sessions, which can often provide the emotional support the addict may need to make it through withdrawal and the post-withdrawal syndrome of negative feelings and poor self-image. These communal homes do not actually cure the addict, but they do get him or her off the drugs while simultaneously providing basic living needs.

Other forms of rational authority treatment use basically the same philosophy of enforced treatment as a therapeutic means of forcing the patient into a strong relationship with another person. These treatments usually involve imposing certain responsibilities and guidelines on the patient with jail as the alternative. Ideally, the patient gradually internalizes these imposed controls and becomes a more responsible person. Although these treatments, like the use of communal homes, fail to cure the addict, they can nurture the responsibility and self-esteem that will make the addict's life more bearable.

All of these treatments have positive qualities. The ideal situation would be to combine the best aspects of each. In fact, many of the current treatments do derive from the philosophies of more than one of these forms of therapy. For example, some methadone maintenance programs, in addition to using pharmacological methods, include psychological principles (such as keeping the addict in a healthy environment) and a degree of authority (threatening the addict with punishment if he or she goes back to heroin). In all cases, the particular needs of each addict must be evaluated and taken into consideration.

This exhibit provides a grim reminder that abuse of opiate narcotics often results in death. There are more than 500,000 narcotics addicts—representing all social classes—in the United States today.

CHAPTER 8

THE CHALLENGE TODAY

Within the United States alone, there are over half a million narcotics addicts. This represents a major social problem, and one that is not likely to be resolved without the three-way cooperation of scientists, physicians, and drug consumers. The researchers' role in combatting addiction has already been discussed. Their job is to discover an effective narcotic that does not cause dependence and does not burden the user with adverse side effects. With the development of the partial agonists scientists have gotten close to this goal. However, it might be impossible for the opiate drugs to exert their analgesic effects without causing some degree of addiction.

With this in mind, it is important to approach other aspects of the addiction problem. One thing that should be done is to re-evaluate the training of physicians. The writing of a prescription is the physician's most common response to a problem, and yet many doctors are ill-prepared to do so intelligently. In testimony before a U.S. Senate committee in 1974, experts claimed that the average doctor in the United States receives very little training in pharmacology in medical school and that much of this training comes in the first year. Furthermore, it was stated that less than 10% of the medical schools in the United States have courses in drug therapeutics.

To fight addiction effectively, especially the accidental type, it is also necessary to educate physicians on the abuse potential of many drugs. Eliminating overprescribing and the writing of unnecessary prescriptions should be a major objective in the battle against narcotics abuse.

Although a great deal of overprescription can arise from a doctor's ignorance, there is also the element of greed. Some doctors supplement their incomes by buying narcotics from the manufacturer and selling them to "patients" who need a fix. These physicians turn a healthy profit, buying drugs such as Dilaudid by the hundreds for $25 to $50 and selling them for a few dollars per tablet. On the street, each Dilaudid tablet may cost $20. The primary offenders in this trade are older doctors who have outlived their clients and younger physicians who have not yet built up a profitable business.

One example of illicit trade involved a Michigan physician who fled the state after his first wife died of a drug overdose and his second wife was physically assaulted by the doctor himself. The physician moved to the South, where he obtained another license and immediately used it to sell 38 illegal prescriptions. He was apprehended but once again fled. Perhaps the most frightening example of the errant physician is Dr. Robert Abbot of Pennsylvania. In the span of just 14 months, he ordered 1.8 million pills and turned over $400,000 in profits before police traced pills from the streets of Baltimore back to him. The 74-year-old Abbot was sentenced to 15 years in jail and received a $90,000 fine.

It should be pointed out that the proportion of these unethical physicians is small—only an estimated 1% to 2% of all professionals who handle drugs take part in these illicit activities. However, these few "bad apples" account for almost half of all illegally channeled prescription drugs in the United States.

Finally, the public must be educated about the drugs they are using. It should be remembered that all drug prescriptions involve the doctor and the patient, and often it is the patient who demands a prescription. The doctor often feels obliged to give the patient something tangible, and thus complies. Education of the patient would reduce the incidence of accidental addiction, because knowledgeable patients can question their doctors and assure themselves that they know what they are getting into. Thus, distribution of basic information on the dangers of narcotics would probably save countless patients from addiction.

The education of the physician and the patient is the least that should be done to fight narcotics abuse, barring the development of a nonaddictive opiate. The need for education was emphasized by the results of a 1989 poll, which found that 8.3% of all high school seniors had recreationally tried a non-heroin opiate. This number is a cause for concern in the face of the addictive potential of narcotics. A person who has tried them once often comes back for more.

Measures must be taken to stem the growing rate of addiction because of its effects on society. The estimate that 50% to 75% of all property crimes are related to narcotics (primarily heroin) is a glaring illustration of this fact. The U.S. gross national product is also hindered by abuse of these drugs. Lunch break has become "pill break" for many workers, and the effects of this can be reflected in the lower productivity of a company.

Although it is easy to see the detrimental effects that narcotics abuse can have on society in general, the true tragedy occurs when creative, healthy lives are unnecessarily destroyed. The crumbling of such lives can be and must be avoided.

Appendix I

POPULATION ESTIMATES OF LIFETIME AND CURRENT NONMEDICAL DRUG USE, 1988

	12-17 years (pop. 20,250,000)			18-25 years (pop. 29,688,000)		
	%	Ever Used	% Current User	%	Ever Used	% Current User
Marijuana & Hashish	17	3,516,000	6 1,296,000	56	16,741,000	16 4,594,000
Hallucinogens	3	704,000	1 168,000	14	4,093,000	2 569,000
Inhalants	9	1,774,000	2 410,000	12	3,707,000	2 514,000
Cocaine	3	683,000	1 225,000	20	5,858,000	5 1,323,000
Crack	1	188,000	+ +	3	1,000,000	1 249,000
Heroin	1	118,000	+ +	+	+	+ +
Stimulants*	4	852,000	1 245,000	1	3,366,000	2 718,000
Sedatives	2	475,000	1 1 23,000	6	1,633,000	1 265,000
Tranquilizers	2	413,000	+ +	8	2,319,000	1 307,000
Analgesics	4	840,000	1 182,000	9	2,798,000	1 440,000
Alcohol	50	10,161,000	25 5,097,000	90	26,807,000	65 19,392,000
Cigarettes	42	8,564,000	12 2,389,000	75	22,251,000	35 10,447,000
Smokeless Tobacco	15	3,021,000	4 722,000	24	6,971,000	6 1,855,000

* Amphetamines and related substances
+ Amounts of less than .5% are not listed
  Terms: Ever Used: used at least once in a person's lifetime.
         Current User: used at least once in the 30 days prior to the survey.

Source: National Institute on Drug Abuse, August 1989

POPULATION ESTIMATES OF LIFETIME AND CURRENT NONMEDICAL DRUG USE, 1988

26+ years (pop. 148,409,000)				TOTAL (pop. 198,347,000)			
%	Ever Used	%	Current User	%	Ever Used	%	Current User
31	45,491,000	4	5,727,000	33	65,748,000	6	11,616,000
7	9,810,000	+	+	7	4,607,000	+	+
4	5,781,000	+	+	6	1,262,000	1	1,223,000
10	14,631,000	1	1,375,000	11	21,171,000	2	2,923,000
+	+	+	+	1	2,483,000	+	484,000
1	1,686,000	+	+	1	1,907,000	+	+
7	9,850,000	1	791,000	7	4,068,000	1	1,755,000
3	4,867,000	+	+	4	6,975,000	+	+
5	6,750,000	1	822,000	5	9,482,000	1	1,174,000
5	6,619,000	+	+	5	10,257,000	1	1,151,000
89	131,530,000	55	81,356,000	85	168,498,000	53	105,845,000
80	118,191,000	30	44,284,000	75	149,005,000	29	57,121,000
13	19,475,000	3	4,497,000	15	29,467,000	4	7,073,000

Appendix II

DRUGS MENTIONED MOST FREQUENTLY BY HOSPITAL EMERGENCY ROOMS, 1988

	Drug name	Number of mentions by emergency rooms	Percent of total number of mentions
1	Cocaine	62,141	38.80
2	Alcohol-in-combination	46,588	29.09
3	Heroin/Morphine	20,599	12.86
4	Marijuana/Hashish	10,722	6.69
5	PCP/PCP Combinations	8,403	5.25
6	Acetaminophen	6,426	4.01
7	Diazepam	6,082	3.80
8	Aspirin	5,544	3.46
9	Ibuprofen	3,878	2.42
10	Alprazolam	3,846	2.40
11	Methamphetamine/Speed	3,030	1.89
12	Acetaminophen W Codeine	2,457	1.53
13	Amitriptyline	1,960	1.22
14	D.T.C. Sleep Aids	1,820	1.14
15	Methadone	1,715	1.07
16	Triazolam	1,640	1.02
17	Diphenhydramine	1,574	0.98
18	D-Propoxyphene	1,563	0.98
19	Hydantoin	1,442	0.90
20	Lorazepam	1,345	0.84
21	LSD	1,317	0.82
22	Amphetamine	1,316	0.82
23	Phenobarbital	1,223	0.76
24	Oxycodone	1,192	0.74
25	Imipramine	1,064	0.66

Source: Drug Abuse Warning Network (DAWN), Annual Data 1988

Appendix III

DRUGS MENTIONED MOST FREQUENTLY BY MEDICAL EXAMINERS (IN AUTOPSY REPORTS), 1988

	Drug name	Number of mentions in autopsy reports	Percent of total number of drug mentions
1	Cocaine	3,308	48.96
2	Alcohol-in-combination	2,596	38.43
3	Heroin/Morphine	2,480	36.71
4	Codeine	689	10.20
5	Diazepam	464	6.87
6	Methadone	447	6.62
7	Amitriptyline	402	5.95
8	Nortriptyline	328	4.85
9	Lidocaine	306	4.53
10	Acetaminophen	293	4.34
11	D-Propoxyphene	271	4.01
12	Marijuana/Hashish	263	3.89
13	Quinine	224	3.32
14	Unspec Benzodiazepine	222	3.29
15	PCP/PCP Combinations	209	3.09
16	Diphenhydramine	192	2.84
17	Phenobarbital	183	2.71
18	Desipramine	177	2.62
19	Methamphetamine/Speed	161	2.38
20	Doxepin	152	2.25
21	Aspirin	138	2.04
22	Imipramine	137	2.03
23	Hydantoin	98	1.45
24	Amphetamine	87	1.29
25	Chlordiazepoxide	76	1.12

Source: Drug Abuse Warning Network (DAWN), Annual Data 1988

Appendix IV

NATIONAL HIGH SCHOOL SENIOR SURVEY, 1975-1989

	High School Senior Survey Trends in Lifetime Prevalence Percent Who Ever Used				
	Class of 1975	Class of 1976	Class of 1977	Class of 1978	Class of 1979
Marijuana/Hashish	47.3	52.8	56.4	59.2	60.4
Inhalants	NA	10.3	11.1	12.0	12.7
Inhalants Adjusted	NA	NA	NA	NA	18.2
Amyl & Butyl Nitrites	NA	NA	NA	NA	11.1
Hallucinogens	16.3	15.1	13.9	14.3	14.1
Hallucinogens Adjusted	NA	NA	NA	NA	17.7
LSD	11.3	11.0	9.8	9.7	9.5
PCP	NA	NA	NA	NA	12.8
Cocaine	9.0	9.7	10.8	12.9	15.4
Crack	NA	NA	NA	NA	NA
Other cocaine	NA	NA	NA	NA	NA
Heroin	2.2	1.8	1.8	1.6	1.1
Other Opiates*	9.0	9.6	10.3	9.9	10.1
Stimulants*	22.3	22.6	23.0	22.9	24.2
Stimulants Adjusted*	NA	NA	NA	NA	NA
Sedatives*	18.2	17.7	17.4	16.0	14.6
Barbiturates*	16.9	16.2	15.6	13.7	11.8
Methaqualone*	8.1	7.8	8.5	7.9	8.3
Tranquilizers*	17.0	16.8	18.0	17.0	16.3
Alcohol	90.4	91.9	92.5	93.1	93.0
Cigarettes	73.6	75.4	75.7	75.3	74.0

Stimulants adjusted to exclude inappropriate reporting of nonprescription stimulants; stimulants = amphetamines and amphetamine-like substances.
*Only use not under a doctor's orders included.

Source: National Institute on Drug Abuse, National High School Senior Survey: "Monitoring the Future," 1989

NATIONAL HIGH SCHOOL SENIOR SURVEY, 1975-1989

High School Senior Survey
Trends in Lifetime Prevalence
Percent Who Ever Used

Class of 1980	Class of 1981	Class of 1982	Class of 1983	Class of 1984	Class of 1985	Class of 1986	Class of 1987	Class of 1988	Class of 1989
60.3	59.5	58.7	57.0	54.9	54.2	50.9	50.2	47.2	43.7
11.9	12.3	12.8	13.6	14.4	15.4	15.9	17.0	16.7	17.6
17.3	17.2	17.7	18.2	18.0	18.1	20.1	18.6	17.5	18.6
11.1	10.1	9.8	8.4	8.1	7.9	8.6	4.7	3.2	3.3
13.3	13.3	12.5	11.9	10.7	10.3	9.7	10.3	8.9	9.4
15.6	15.3	14.3	13.6	12.3	12.1	11.9	10.6	9.2	9.9
9.3	9.8	9.6	8.9	8.0	7.5	7.2	8.4	7.7	8.3
9.6	7.8	6.0	5.6	5.0	4.9	4.8	3.0	2.9	3.9
15.7	16.5	16.0	16.2	16.1	17.3	16.9	15.2	12.1	10.3
NA	NA	NA	NA	NA	NA	NA	5.4	4.8	4.7
NA	NA	NA	NA	NA	NA	NA	14.0	12.1	8.5
1.1	1.1	1.2	1.2	1.3	1.2	1.1	1.2	1.1	1.3
9.8	10.1	9.6	9.4	9.7	10.2	9.0	9.2	8.6	8.3
26.4	32.2	35.6	35.4	NA	NA	NA	NA	NA	NA
NA	NA	27.9	26.9	27.9	26.2	23.4	21.6	19.8	19.1
14.9	16.0	15.2	14.4	13.3	11.8	10.4	8.7	7.8	7.4
11.0	11.3	10.3	9.9	9.9	9.2	8.4	7.4	6.7	6.5
9.5	10.6	10.7	10.1	8.3	6.7	5.2	4.0	3.3	2.7
15.2	14.7	14.0	13.3	12.4	11.9	10.9	10.9	9.4	7.6
93.2	92.6	92.8	92.6	92.6	92.2	91.3	92.2	92.0	90.7
71.0	71.0	70.1	70.6	69.7	68.8	67.6	67.2	66.4	65.7

Appendix V

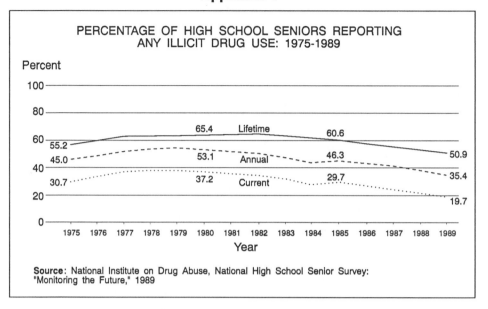

PERCENTAGE OF HIGH SCHOOL SENIORS REPORTING
ANY ILLICIT DRUG USE: 1975-1989

Percent

Source: National Institute on Drug Abuse, National High School Senior Survey: "Monitoring the Future," 1989

Appendix VI

DRUG ABUSE AND AIDS

An estimated 25 percent of all cases of acquired immunodeficiency syndrome, or AIDS, are intravenous (IV) drug abusers. This group is the second largest at risk for AIDS, exceeded only by homosexual, and bisexual men. And the numbers may be growing. Data for the first half of 1988 show that IV drug abusers made up about 31 percent of the total reported cases.

". . . the number of IV drug users with AIDS is doubling every 14-16 months."

According to the National Institute on Drug Abuse (NIDA). There are 1.1 to 1.3 million IV drug users in the United States, and, so far, about 17,500 have developed AIDS. Thousands more are infected with the virus that causes this fatal illness, which kills by destroying the body's ability to fight disease.

Currently, the number of IV drug users with AIDS is doubling every 14-16 months. Although the numbers of IV drug users who carry the AIDS virus varies from region to region, in some places the majority may already be infected. In New York City, for example, 60 percent of IV drug users entering treatment programs have the AIDS virus.

Among IV drug abusers, the AIDS virus is spread primarily by needle sharing. As long as IV drug abusers are drug dependent, they are likely to engage in needle sharing. Thus, the key to eliminating needle sharing—and the associated spread of AIDS—is drug abuse treatment to curb drug dependence. NIDA is working to find ways to get more IV users into treatment and to develop new methods to fight drug addiction. Most non-drug users characteristically associate heroin with IV drug use. However, thousands of others inject cocaine or amphetamines. Recent evidence suggests that IV cocaine use is increasing and that the AIDS virus is spreading in those users. One reason for this may be because cocaine's effects last only a short time. When the drug, which is a stimulant, wears off, users may inject again and again, sharing a needle many times in a few hours. In contrast, heroin users inject once and fall asleep.

". . . IV cocaine use is increasing and the AIDS
virus is spreading in those users."

The apparent increase in IV cocaine is especially worrisome, drug abuse experts say, because there are no standard therapies for treating cocaine addiction. Until scientists find effective treatments for this problem, the ability to control the spread of AIDS will be hampered.

TRANSMISSION

Needle Sharing -- Among IV drug users, transmission of AIDS virus most often occurs by sharing needles, syringes, or other "works." Small amounts of contaminated blood left in the equipment can carry the virus from user to user. IV drug abusers who frequent "shooting galleries" — where paraphernalia is passed among several people -- are at especially high risk for AIDS. But, needle sharing of any sort (at parties, for example) can transmit the virus, and NIDA experts note that almost all IV drug users share needles at one time or another.
Because not every IV drug abuser will enter treatment and because some must wait to be treated, IV users in many cities are being taught to flush their "works" with bleach before they inject. Used correctly, bleach can destroy virus left in the equipment.

Sexual Transmission -- IV drug abusers also get AIDS through unprotected sex with someone who is infected. In addition, the AIDS virus can be sexually transmitted from infected IV drug abusers to individuals who do not use drugs. Data from the Centers for Disease Control show that IV drug use is associated with the increased spread of AIDS in the heterosexual population. For example, of all women reported to have AIDS, 49 percent were IV drug users, while another 30 percent -- non-IV drug users themselves -- were sexual partners of IV drug users. Infected women who become pregnant can pass the AIDS virus to their babies. About 70 percent of all children born with AIDS have had a mother or father who shot drugs.

Non-IV Drug Use and AIDS -- Sexual activity has also been reported as the means of AIDS transmission among those who use non-IV drugs (like crack or marijuana). Many people, especially women, addicted to crack (or other substances) go broke supporting their habit and turn to trading sex for drugs. Another link between substance abuse and AIDS is when individuals using alcohol and drugs relax their restraints and caution regarding sexual behavior. People who normally practice "safe" sex may neglect to do so while "under the influence."

Source: U.S. Public Health Service, AIDS Program Office, 1989

Appendix VII

U.S. Drug Schedules*

	Drugs Included	Dispensing Regulations
Schedule I high potential for abuse; no currently accepted medical use in treatment in U.S.; safety not proven for medical use	heroin methaqualone LSD mescaline peyote phencyclidine analogs psilocybin marijuana hashish	research use only
Schedule II high potential for abuse; currently accepted U.S. medical use; abuse may lead to severe psychological or physical dependence	opium morphine methadone barbiturates cocaine amphetamines phencyclidine codeine	written Rx; no refills
Schedule III less potential for abuse than drugs in Schedules I and II; currently accepted U.S. medical use; may lead to moderate or low physical dependence or high psychological dependence	glutethimide selected morphine, opium, and codeine compounds selected depressant sedative compounds selected stimulants for weight control	written or oral Rx; refills allowed
Schedule IV low potential for abuse relative to drugs in Schedule III; currently accepted U.S. medical use; abuse may lead to limited physical dependence or psychological dependence relative to drugs in Schedule III	selected barbiturate and other depressant compounds selected stimulants for weight control	written or oral Rx; refills allowed
Schedule V low potential for abuse relative to drugs in Schedule IV; currently accepted U.S. medical use; abuse may lead to limited physical dependence or psychological dependence relative to drugs in Schedule IV	selected narcotic compounds	OTC/ M.D.'s order

*Established by the U.S. Controlled Substances Act of 1970
Source: U.S. Drug Enforcement Administration

Appendix VIII

Agencies for the Prevention and Treatment of Drug Abuse

Alabama
Department of Mental Health
Division of Substance Abuse
200 Interstate Park Drive
P.O. Box 3710
Montgomery, AL 36109
(205) 270-9650

Alaska
Department of Health and
  Social Services
Division of Alcoholism and
  Drug Abuse
P.O. Box H
Juneau, AK 99811-0607
(907) 586-6201

Arizona
Department of Health
  Services
Division of Behavioral Health
  Services
Bureau of Community
  Services
The Office of Substance
  Abuse
2632 East Thomas
Phoenix, AZ 85016
(602) 255-1030

Arkansas
Department of Human
  Services
Division of Alcohol and Drug
  Abuse
400 Donagy Plaza North
P.O. Box 1437
Slot 2400
Little Rock, AR 72203-1437
(501) 682-6656

California
Health and Welfare Agencies
Department of Alcohol and
  Drug Programs
1700 K Street
Sacramento, CA 95814-4037
(916) 445-1943

Colorado
Department of Health
Alcohol and Drug Abuse
  Division
4210 East 11th Avenue
Denver, CO 80220
(303) 331-8201

Connecticut
Alcohol and Drug Abuse
  Commission
999 Asylum Avenue
3rd Floor
Hartford, CT 06105
(203) 566-4145

Delaware
Division of Mental Health
Bureau of Alcoholism and
  Drug Abuse
1901 North Dupont Highway
Newcastle, DE 19720
(302) 421-6101

District of Columbia
Department of Human
  Services
Office of Health Planning and
  Development
1660 L Street NW
Room 715
Washington, DC 20036
(202) 724-5641

Florida
Department of Health and
  Rehabilitative Services
Alcohol, Drug Abuse, and
  Mental Health Office
1317 Winewood Boulevard
Building 6, Room 183
Tallahassee, FL 32399-0700
(904) 488-8304

Georgia
Department of Human
  Resources
Division of Mental Health,
  Mental Retardation, and
  Substance Abuse
Alcohol and Drug Section
878 Peachtree Street
Suite 319
Atlanta, GA 30309-3917
(404) 894-4785

Hawaii
Department of Health
Mental Health Division
Alcohol and Drug Abuse
  Branch
1270 Queen Emma Street
Room 706
Honolulu, HI 96813
(808) 548-4280

Idaho
Department of Health and
  Welfare
Bureau of Preventive
  Medicine
Substance Abuse Section
450 West State
Boise, ID 83720
(208) 334-5934

Illinois
Department of Alcoholism
  and Substance Abuse
Illinois Center
100 West Randolph Street
Suite 5-600
Chicago, IL 60601
(312) 814-3840

Indiana
Department of Mental Health
Division of Addiction Services
117 East Washington Street
Indianapolis, IN 46204-3647
(317) 232-7816

Iowa
Department of Public Health
Division of Substance Abuse
Lucas State Office Building
321 East 12th Street
Des Moines, IA 50319
(515) 281-3641

Kansas
Department of Social
  Rehabilitation
Alcohol and Drug Abuse
  Services
300 SW Oakley
2nd Floor
Biddle Building
Topeka, KS 66606
(913) 296-3925

Kentucky
Cabinet for Human Resources
Department of Health
  Services
Substance Abuse Branch
275 East Main Street
Frankfort, KY 40621
(502) 564-2880

Louisiana
Department of Health and
  Hospitals
Office of Human Services
Division of Alcohol and Drug
  Abuse
P.O. Box 3868
Baton Rouge, LA 70821-3868
1201 Capital Access Road
Baton Rouge, LA 70802
(504) 342-9354

Maine
Department of Human
  Services
Office of Alcoholism and
  Drug Abuse Prevention
Bureau of Rehabilitation
5 Anthony Avenue
State House, Station 11
Augusta, ME 04433
(207) 289-2781

Maryland
Alcohol and Drug Abuse
  Administration
201 West Preston Street

4th Floor
Baltimore, MD 21201
(301) 225-6910

Massachusetts
Department of Public Health
Division of Substance Abuse
150 Tremont Street
Boston, MA 02111
(617) 727-1960

Michigan
Department of Public Health
Office of Substance Abuse
  Services
2150 Apollo Drive
P.O. Box 30206
Lansing, MI 48909
(517) 335-8810

Minnesota
Department of Human
  Services
Chemical Dependency
  Division
444 Lafayette Road
St. Paul, MN 55155
(612) 296-4614

Mississippi
Department of Mental Health
Division of Alcohol and Drug
  Abuse
1101 Robert E. Lee Building
239 North Lamar Street
Jackson, MS 39201
(601) 359-1288

Missouri
Department of Mental
  Health
Division of Alcoholism and
  Drug Abuse
1706 East Elm Street
P.O. Box 687
Jefferson City, MO 65102
(314) 751-4942

Montana
Department of Institutions
Alcohol and Drug Abuse
  Division
1539 11th Avenue
Helena, MT 59620
(406) 444-2827

Nebraska
Department of Public
  Institutions
Division of Alcoholism and
  Drug Abuse
801 West Van Dorn Street
P.O. Box 94728
Lincoln, NB 68509-4728
(402) 471-2851, Ext. 5583

Nevada
Department of Human
  Resources
Bureau of Alcohol and Drug
  Abuse
505 East King Street
Room 500
Carson City, NV 89710
(702) 687-4790

New Hampshire
Department of Health and
  Human Services
Office of Alcohol and Drug
  Abuse Prevention
State Office
Park South
105 Pleasant Street
Concord, NH 03301
(603) 271-6100

New Jersey
Department of Health
Division of Alcoholism and
  Drug Abuse
129 East Hanover Street CN
  362
Trenton, NJ 08625
(609) 292-8949

New Mexico
Health and Environment
  Department
Behavioral Health Services
  Division/
Substance Abuse
Harold Runnels Building
1190 Saint Francis Drive
Santa Fe, NM 87503
(505) 827-2601

New York
Division of Alcoholism and
  Alcohol Abuse
194 Washington Avenue

Albany, NY 12210
(518) 474-5417

Division of Substance Abuse
Services
Executive Park South
Box 8200
Albany, NY 12203
(518) 457-7629

North Carolina
Department of Human
Resources
Division of Mental Health,
Developmental Disabilities,
and Substance Abuse
Services
Alcohol and Drug Abuse
Services
325 North Salisbury Street
Albemarle Building
Raleigh, NC 27603
(919) 733-4670

North Dakota
Department of Human Services
Division of Alcohol and Drug
Abuse
1839 East Capital Avenue
Bismarck, ND 58501-2152
(701) 224-2769

Ohio
Division of Alcohol and Drug
Addiction Services
246 North High Street
3rd Floor
Columbus, OH 43266-0170
(614) 466-3445

Oklahoma
Department of Mental Health
and Substance Abuse
Services
Alcohol and Drug Abuse
Services
1200 North East 13th Street
P.O. Box 53277
Oklahoma City, OK 73152-
3277
(405) 271-8653

Oregon
Department of Human
Resources

Office of Alcohol and Drug
Abuse Programs
1178 Chemeketa NE
#102
Salem, OR 97310
(503) 378-2163

Pennsylvania
Department of Health
Office of Drug and Alcohol
Programs
Health and Welfare Building
Room 809
P.O. Box 90
Harrisburg, PA 17108
(717) 787-9857

Rhode Island
Department of Mental Health,
Mental Retardation and
Hospitals
Division of Substance Abuse
Substance Abuse
Administration Building
P.O. Box 20363
Cranston, RI 02920
(401) 464-2091

South Carolina
Commission on Alcohol and
Drug Abuse
3700 Forest Drive
Suite 300
Columbia, SC 29204
(803) 734-9520

South Dakota
Department of Human Services
700 Governor's Drive
Pier South D
Pierre, SD 57501-2291
(605) 773-4806

Tennessee
Department of Mental Health
and Mental Retardation
Alcohol and Drug Abuse
Services
706 Church Street
Nashville, TN 37243-0675
(615) 741-1921

Texas
Commission on Alcohol and
Drug Abuse

720 Bracos Street
Suite 403
Austin, TX 78701
(512) 463-5510

Utah
Department of Social Services
Division of Substance Abuse
120 North 200 West
4th Floor
Salt Lake City, UT 84103
(801) 538-3939

Vermont
Agency of Human Services
Department of Social and
Rehabilitation Services
Office of Alcohol and Drug
Abuse Programs
103 South Main Street
Waterbury, VT 05676
(802) 241-2170

Virginia
Department of Mental Health
and Mental Retardation
Division of Substance Abuse
109 Governor Street
8th Floor
P.O. Box 1797
Richmond, VA 23214
(804) 786-5313

Washington
Department of Social and
Health Service
Division of Alcohol and
Substance Abuse
12th and Franklin
Mail Stop OB 21W
Olympia, WA 98504
(206) 753-5866

West Virginia
Department of Health and
Human Resources
Office of Behavioral Health
Services
Division on Alcoholism and
Drug Abuse
Capital Complex
1900 Kanawha Boulevard East
Building 3, Room 402
Charleston, WV 25305
(304) 348-2276

Wisconsin

Department of Health and
Social Services
Division of Community
Services
Bureau of Community
Programs
Office of Alcohol and Drug
Abuse
1 West Wilson Street
P.O. Box 7851
Madison, WI 53707-7851
(608) 266-2717

Wyoming

Alcohol And Drug Abuse
Programs
451 Hathaway Building
Cheyenne, WY 82002
(307) 777-7115

U.S. TERRITORIES AND POSSESSIONS

American Samoa

LBJ Tropical Medical Center
Department of Mental Health
Clinic
Pago Pago, American Samoa
96799

Guam

Mental Health & Substance
Abuse Agency
P.O. Box 20999
Guam 96921

Puerto Rico

Department of Addiction
Control Services
Alcohol and Drug Abuse
Programs
Avenida Barbosa
P.O. Box 414
Rio Piedras, PR 00928-1474
(809) 763-7575

Trust Territories

Director of Health Services
Office of the High
Commissioner
Saipan, Trust Territories
96950

Virgin Islands

Division of Health and
Substance Abuse
Becastro Building
3rd Street, Sugar Estate
St. Thomas, Virgin Islands
00802

CANADA

Canadian Centre on
Substance Abuse
112 Kent Street, Suite 480
Ottawa, Ontario
K1P 5P2
(613) 235-4048

Alberta

Alberta Alcohol and Drug
Abuse Commission
10909 Jasper Avenue, 6th
Floor
Edmonton, Alberta
T5J 3M9
(403) 427-2837

British Columbia

Ministry of Labour and
Consumer Services
Alcohol and Drug Programs
1019 Wharf Street, 5th Floor
Victoria, British Columbia
V8V 1X4
(604) 387-5870

Manitoba

The Alcoholism Foundation of
Manitoba
1031 Portage Avenue
Winnipeg, Manitoba
R3G 0R8
(204) 944-6226

New Brunswick

Alcoholism and Drug
Dependency Commission
of New Brunswick
65 Brunswick Street
P.O. Box 6000
Fredericton, New Brunswick
E3B 5H1
(506) 453-2136

Newfoundland

The Alcohol and Drug
Dependency Commission
of Newfoundland and
Labrador
Suite 105, Prince Charles
Building
120 Torbay Road, 1st Floor
St. John's, Newfoundland
A1A 2G8
(709) 737-3600

Northwest Territories

Alcohol and Drug Services
Department of Social Services
Government of Northwest
Territories
Box 1320 - 52nd Street
6th Floor, Precambrian
Building
Yellowknife, Northwest
Territories
S1A 2L9
(403) 920-8005

Nova Scotia

Nova Scotia Commission on
Drug Dependency
6th Floor, Lord Nelson
Building
5675 Spring Garden Road
Halifax, Nova Scotia
B3J 1H1
(902) 424-4270

Ontario

Addiction Research
Foundation
33 Russell Street
Toronto, Ontario
M5S 2S1
(416) 595-6000

Prince Edward Island

Addiction Services of Prince
Edward Island
P.O. Box 37
Eric Found Building
65 McGill Avenue
Charlottetown, Prince Edward
Island
C1A 7K2
(902) 368-4120

Quebec

Service des Programmes aux
Personnes Toxicomanie
Gouvernement du Quebec
Ministere de la Sante et des
Services Sociaux
1005 Chemin Ste. Foy
Quebec City, Quebec
G1S 4N4
(418) 643-9887

Saskatchewan

Saskatchewan Alcohol and
Drug Abuse Commission
1942 Hamilton Street
Regina, Saskatchewan
S4P 3V7
(306) 787-4085

Yukon

Alcohol and Drug Services
Department of Health and
Social Resources
Yukon Territorial
Government
6118-6th Avenue
P.O. Box 2703
Whitehorse, Yukon Territory
Y1A 2C6
(403) 667-5777

Paul R. Sanberg, Ph.D., is a professor of psychiatry, psychology, neurosurgery, physiology, and biophysics at the University of Cincinnati College of Medicine. Currently, he is also a professor of psychiatry at Brown University and scientific director for Cellular Transplants, Inc., in Providence, Rhode Island.

Professor Sanberg has held research positions at the Australian National University at Canberra, the Johns Hopkins University School of Medicine, and Ohio University. He has written many journal articles and book chapters in the fields of neuroscience and psychopharmacology. He has served on the editorial boards of many scientific journals and is the recipient of numerous awards.

Michael D. Bunsey has a B.S. degree in psychology from Ohio University and a doctorate in biopsychology from Cornell University.

Solomon H. Snyder, M.D., is Distinguished Service Professor of Neuroscience, Pharmacology and Psychiatry at the Johns Hopkins University School of Medicine. He has served as president of the Society for Neuroscience and in 1978 received the Albert Lasker Award in Medical Research. He has authored *Drugs and the Brain, Uses of Marijuana, Madness and the Brain, The Troubled Mind,* and *Biological Aspects of Mental Disorder* and has edited *Perspectives in Neuropharmacology: A Tribute to Julius Axelrod.* Professor Snyder was a research associate with Dr. Axelrod at the National Institutes of Health.

Barry L. Jacobs, Ph.D., is currently a professor in the neuroscience program at Princeton University. Professor Jacobs is the author of *Serotonin Neurotransmission and Behavior* and *Hallucinogens: Neurochemical, Behavioral and Clinical Perspectives.* He has written many journal articles in the field of neuroscience and contributed numerous chapters to books on behavior and brain science. He has been a member of several panels of the National Institute of Mental Health.

Jerome H. Jaffe, M.D., formerly professor of psychiatry at the College of Physicians and Surgeons, Columbia University, is director of the Addiction Research Center of the National Institute on Drug Abuse. Dr. Jaffe is also a psychopharmacologist and has conducted research on a wide range of addictive drugs and developed treatment programs for addicts. He has acted as special consultant to the president on narcotics and dangerous drugs and was the first director of the White House Special Action Office for Drug Abuse Prevention.

Further Reading

General

Berger, Gilda. *Drug Abuse: The Impact on Society*. New York: Watts, 1988. (Gr. 7–12)

Cohen, Susan, and Daniel Cohen. *What You Can Believe About Drugs: An Honest and Unhysterical Guide for Teens*. New York: M. Evans, 1987. (Gr. 7–12)

Musto, David F. *The American Disease: Origins of Narcotic Control*. Rev. ed. New Haven: Yale University Press, 1987.

National Institute on Drug Abuse. *Drug Use, Drinking, and Smoking: National Survey Results from High School, College, and Young Adult Populations, 1975–1988*. Washington, DC: Public Health Service, Department of Health and Human Services, 1989.

O'Brien, Robert, and Sidney Cohen. *Encyclopedia of Drug Abuse*. New York: Facts on File, 1984.

Snyder, Solomon H., M.D. *Drugs and the Brain*. New York: Scientific American Books, 1986.

U.S. Department of Justice. *Drugs of Abuse*. 1989 ed. Washington, DC: Government Printing Office, 1989.

Prescription Narcotics

Casy, Alan, F., and Robert Parfitt. *Opioid Analgesics*. New York: Plenum, 1986.

Kihar, Michael J., and Gavril W. Pasternak, eds. *Analgesics: Neurochemical, Behavioral, and Clinical Perspectives*. New York: Raven Press, 1984.

Long, James W., M.D. *The Essential Guide to Prescription Drugs, 1991*. New York: HarperCollins, 1991.

The Physicians' Desk Reference for Prescription Drugs. Oradell, NJ: Medical Economics, 1991.

The Pill Book. 4th ed. New York: Bantam Books, 1990.

Restak, Richard, M.D. *The Mind*. New York: Bantam Books, 1988.

Rodgers, Joann. *Drugs and Pain*. New York: Chelsea House, 1987. (Gr. 7–12)

Glossary

acetaminophen a minor pain reliever not containing aspirin

acupuncture a Far Eastern technique for treating pain or disease or for inhibiting sensation by passing long needles through the skin at specific points of the body

addiction a condition caused by repeated drug use and characterized by a compulsive urge to continue using the drug, a tendency to increase the dosage, and physiological and/or psychological dependence

AIDS acquired immune deficiency syndrome; an acquired defect in the immune system; the final stage of the disease caused by the human immunodeficiency virus (HIV); spread by the exchange of blood (including contaminated hypodermic needles), by sexual contact, through nutritive fluids passed from a mother to her fetus, and through breast-feeding; leaves victims vulnerable to certain, often fatal, infections and cancers

amino acid an organic chemical compound that is the building block of protein

analgesic a drug that produces an insensitivity to pain without loss of consciousness

angina pectoris a disease marked by chest pains caused by a lack of oxygen to the heart muscles

antihistamine a drug that inhibits the action of histamine and thus reduces the allergic response

antitussive substances that act to inhibit an uncontrollable, dry, or unproductive cough

anxiety an emotional state caused by uncertainty, apprehension, fear, and/or dread that produces such symptoms as sweating, agitation, and increased blood pressure and heart rate

anxiolytics anti-anxiety drugs

cerebral cortex the part of the brain that is the seat of consciousness and the center of memory, learning, reasoning, judgment, and intelligence

codeine a sedative and pain-relieving agent found in opium and related to, but less potent than, morphine

cross-tolerance a condition of tolerance to one or more drugs caused by the body's tolerance to another drug

dependence a psychological craving for a drug that may or may not be accompanied by physical addiction

depression a sometimes overwhelming emotional state characterized by feelings of inadequacy and hopelessness and accompanied by a decrease in physical and psychological activity

dysphoria an exaggerated feeling of being unwell characteristic of depression; opposite of euphoria *endorphins* chemicals found in the brain and recognized as the body's own painkillers, which act in a manner similar to morphine and codeine

enkephalins peptides found predominantly in the brain; they can cause analgesia, physical dependence, and central nervous system depression

enzyme a protein that acts as a catalyst to chemical reactions

euphoria a mental high characterized by a sense of well-being

heroin a semisynthetic opiate produced by a chemical modification of morphine

hypothermia a condition characterized by lower-than-normal body temperature

limbic system a network of structure—including the hippocampus, amygdala, and hypothalamus—in the forebrain; thought to be the center of emotions

methadone a synthetic drug similar to morphine and used for the treatment of relatively severe pain

morphine the principal psychoactive ingredient of opium which produces sleep or a state of stupor; the standard against which all morphinelike drugs are compared

myocardial infarction cardiac failure (heart attack) resulting from lack of blood to a portion of the heart

narcotic originally, a group of drugs producing effects similar to morphine; often used to refer to any substance that sedates, has a depressive effect, and/or causes dependence

neuron a specialized cell, composed of axons, dendrites, and a cell body, which carries electrical messages and is the structural unit of the nervous system

neurotransmitter a chemical, such as ACh, that travels from the axon of one neuron, across the synaptic gap, and to the receptor on an adjacent dendrite, thus allowing communication between neural cells

nociceptors pain receptors

opiate compound from the milky juice of the poppy plant *Papaver somniferum*, including opium, morphine, codeine, and their derivatives, such as heroin

opiate agonist a drug, such as morphine, which, when administered, increases the effects of an opiate

opiate antagonist a drug that, when administered, prevents an opiate from producing its characteristic effect

opium an addictive narcotic drug that consists of the dried juice of the opium poppy plant

overdose   a dose of a drug sufficient to cause an acute reaction such as coma, hysteria, or even death

peptide   a compound containing two or more amino acids

pharmacodynamic tolerance   the increasing tolerance of the nervous system to a drug

physical dependence   adaptation of body to the presence of a drug such that its absence produces withdrawal symptoms

pituitary gland   gland that produces various hormones that regulate such bodily functions as growth and reproduction

placebo effect   a pharmacological effect on a symptom produced by a substance either pharmacologically inert or active only in the treatment of unrelated symptoms

psychological dependence   a condition in which the drug user craves a drug to maintain a sense of well-being and feels discomfort when deprived of it

rebound effect   the appearance, due to the discontinuation of a drug, of a symptom that is opposite to that drug's normal effect

receptor   a specialized component of a cell that combines with a chemical substance to alter the function of the cell; for example, nerve-cell receptors combine with neurotransmitters

SIDS   sudden infant death syndrome; death due to unknown causes of an infant in apparently good health; also called crib death

somatic pain   pain that occurs in the bones or skeletal muscles

synthesize   to create a chemical compound by combining elements or simpler compounds or by degrading a complex compound; generally refers to a laboratory process

thalamus   the part of the brain that receives pain messages and then relays them to other parts of the brain

tolerance   a decrease of susceptibility to the effects of a drug due to its continued administration, resulting in the user's need to increase the drug dosage in order to achieve the effects experienced previously

vasodilation   dilation of a blood vessel

visceral pain   pain that occurs in an organ of the body

withdrawal   the physiological and psychological effects of discontinued use of a drug

Index

Abbot, Robert, 90
Acupuncture, 53
A-delta fibers, 29. *See also* Pain
Alcohol, 20, 47. *See also* Narcotics,
prescription: interactions with
other drugs
Al Rhazi, 31. *See also* Opiates: history
Analgesics, 21–22. *See also* Narcotics,
prescription: analgesic effects
Anxiolytics, 40
Avicenna, 31. *See also* Opiates: history
Baudelaire, Charles, 21
Beta-endorphin, 52. *See also* Opiates:
endogenous
"Blue Velvet," 63. *See also* Narcotics,
prescription: slang names
British East India Company, 31–32. *See
also* Opiates: history
Browning, Elizabeth Barrett, 21
Butorphanol (Stadol), 75–77. *See also*
Opiates: partial agonists
Caffeine, 65, 68
Cerebral cortex, 29. *See also* Narcotics,
prescription: central nervous
system effects
C fibers, 29. *See also* Pain
Codeine, 33, 42, 65. *See also* Opiates
Coleridge, Samuel Taylor, 21
Controlled Substances Act, 59, 67. *See
also* Drug schedules; Narcotics,
prescription: legal status
Cross-tolerance, 46, 80. *See also*
Narcotics, prescription: addiction
Darvon. *See* Propoxyphene
DAWN. *See* Drug Abuse Warning Network
Demerol. *See* Meperidine
Dilaudid. *See* Hydromorphone
Dolophine. *See* Methadone
Doriden, 66. *See also* Narcotics,
prescription: interactions with
other drugs
Drug Abuse Warning Network (DAWN), 66
Drug dependence, 43–44, 64. *See also*
Narcotics, prescription: addiction
Drug schedules, 59, 63, 66, 67, 72. *See
also* Narcotics, prescription:
legal status
Dumas, Alexandre, 21

Endorphins, 51–53, 56. *See also* Opiates:
endogenous
Enforced treatment, 86–87. *See also*
Narcotics, prescription: addiction
Enkephalins, 51–52. *See also* Opiates:
endogenous
Enzymes, 55–56. *See also* Narcotics,
prescription: mechanisms of
action
Food and Drug Administration (FDA), 68.
See also Narcotics, prescription:
legal status
"4s and Dors," 66. *See also* Narcotics,
prescription: slang names
Galen, 31. *See also* Opiates: history
Gautier, Théophile, 21
Heroin, 35–37, 59, 63, 69, 82, 84, 87. *See
also* Opiates
Hydrocodone, 73. *See also* Opiates
Hydromorphone (Dilaudid), 73–74, 90.
See also Opiates
"Kick," 42. *See also* Narcotics,
prescription: central nervous
system effects
Kubla Khan (Coleridge), 21
LAAM, 82, 85. *See also* Narcotics,
prescription: addiction
Laudanum, 21, 31. *See also* Opium
Leu-enkephalin, 52. *See also* Opiates:
endogenous
Levorphanol (Levo-Dromeran), 72–73
Limbic system, 29, 49. *See also* Narcotics,
prescription: central nervous
system effects
Maintenance. *See* Methadone: treatment of
narcotics addiction
MAO inhibitors, 71. *See also* Narcotics,
prescription: interactions with
other drugs
Marijuana, 21
Medical professionals
abuse of narcotics, 36–37
role in prescribing narcotics, 19–20,
44, 89–90
Meperidine (Demerol), 37, 71, 75. *See
also* Opiates
Met-enkephalin, 52. *See also* Opiates:
endogenous

Methadone, 45, 69–70
    treament for narcotics addiction, 69,
        79–87. *See also* Narcotics,
        prescription: addiction;
        Narcotics, prescription: opiates
Morphine, 21, 44, 50, 64, 85
    abuse, 33, 64–65
    compared to other opiates, 32,
        65–66, 69, 71–77
    medical uses, 64
Nalbuphine (Nubain), 77. *See also*
        Opiates: partial agonists
Naloxone, 75, 77, 84. *See also* Opiates:
        antagonists
Naltrexone, 86. *See also* Opiates:
        antagonists
Narcotics, prescription
    abuse potential, 22, 33, 60, 63–77,
        82, 91
    addiction
        causes, 36, 55–57
        classification, 43–44
        detrimental effects, 20, 22, 47, 60,
            91
        examples, 19–21, 37
        history, 31–35, 37
        medical professionals and, 19–20,
            23, 36–37, 89–90
        prevention, 22–23, 89–91
        treatment, 21, 69, 79–87
    analgesic effects, 19–22, 25–26, 29,
        39–40, 59–60, 61–62, 64,
        69–77, 89
    cardiovascular system effects, 42, 47,
        75–77
    central nervous system effects,
        20–21, 39–42, 47, 60–61,
        65–66, 69–71, 74–77
    characteristics of abusers, 34–36
    considerations in prescribing, 23, 46,
        60, 75, 89–90
    deaths, 47, 66, 69, 70, 82–83
    definition, 21, 39
    gastrointestinal system effects, 41
    interactions with other drugs, 20, 40,
        47, 60, 63, 66–67, 69, 71, 75
    legal status, 59, 61–62, 66, 67–69
    long-term effects, 42–44
    mechanisms of action, 39, 49–51,
        54–57

    medical uses, 19, 33–34, 39–42, 59,
        61–66, 69–77
    overdose, 21–22, 47, 61, 66–69, 72,
        82
    pregnancy and, 59, 61, 70, 76–77
    respiratory system effects, 40, 42, 47,
        61, 66, 74, 77
    risks, 21, 40, 42, 47 60–62
    routes of administration, 31, 33, 65,
        69–71, 87
    side effects, 40–42, 64–66, 70–77
    slang names, 64–66, 68, 75
    tolerance, 46–47, 54–57, 71
    trade names, 66, 68, 70–75, 77
    withdrawal, 20, 44–46, 50, 54–57,
        61, 74–77, 84. *See also* Opiates
Neurons, 28, 50, 55
Neurotransmitters, 49, 55
Nociceptors, 28. *See also* Pain
Nubain. *See* Nalbuphine
Opiates
    agonists, 50, 61–74
    antagonists, 50, 53–54, 75, 82–85
    endogenous, 51–54, 56
    history, 21, 30–37
    natural, 21
    partial agonists, 74–77, 89
    receptors, 49, 51, 56
    sources, 21
    synthetic, 21. *See also* Narcotics,
        prescription
Opium, 21, 31–32, 61–62. *See also*
        Opiates
Opium poppy (*Papaver somniferum*), 21
Opium Wars, 32. *See also* Opiates: history
Oxycodone, 71–72. *See also* Opiates
Oxymorphone (Numorphan), 72, 77. *See
        also* Opiates
Pain
    emotion and, 26, 39–40, 49
    factors influencing, 26–28
    function, 25
    kinds of, 25–26, 39
    neurological basis, 28–29
    phantom, 26–27
    treatment, 29, 59–60. *See also*
        Narcotics, prescription: analgesic
        effects; Narcotics, prescription:
        medical uses
Papaver somniferum. *See* Opium poppy

Paracelsus, 31. *See also* Opiates: history

Paregoric, 34, 61–62. *See also* Opiates

Pentazocine (Talwin), 74–75. *See also* Opiates: partial agonists

Percodan, 19–20, 72. *See also* Oxycodone

Pharmacological treatment, 79–86. *See also* Narcotics, prescription: addiction

Phenacetin, 65, 68. *See also* Analgesics

Pituitary gland, 52

Placebo effect, 53–54. *See also* Narcotics, prescription: mechanisms of action

Poe, Edgar Allan, 21

Propoxyphene (Darvon), 47, 66–68. *See also* Opiates

Psychotherapy, 79. *See also* Narcotics, prescription: addiction

Pure Food and Drug Act, 35. *See also* Narcotics, prescription: legal status

Rational authority treatment, 86. *See also* Narcotics, prescription: addiction

Rebound effect, 41. *See also* Narcotics, prescription: side effects

"Rush," 42, 63. *See also* Narcotics, prescription: central nervous system effects

Serturner, Frederick, 32

Stadol. *See* Butorphanol

STEPS method, 84–85. *See also* Narcotics, prescription: addiction

Syndenham, Thomas, 21. *See also* Opiates: history

Talwin. *See* Pentazocine

Thalamus, 29, 49. *See also* Narcotics, prescription: central nervous system effects

Theophrastus, 31. *See also* Opiates: history

Tolerance, 46. *See also* Narcotics, prescription: addiction

"Ts and Blues," 75. *See also* Narcotics, prescription: slang names

Tylenol, 66. *See also* Analgesics

Withdrawal, 44–46. *See also* Narcotics, prescription: withdrawal

Wolfe, Sidney, 67

Wood, Alexander, 33